FROM
BELSEN
TO BUCKINGHAM PALACE

Paul Oppenheimer

FROM
BELSEN
TO BUCKINGHAM PALACE

By Paul Oppenheimer

Published in Great Britain by
Quill Press
P.O. Box 2002,
Newark, Nottinghamshire. NG22 9ZG

© 1996 Paul Oppenheimer
First published by Beth Shalom, September 1996
Reprinted September 1997, July 1999
Republished by Quill Press, August 2000
Reprinted November 2001, January 2004, December 2004,
August 2005

British Library Catalogue in Publication Data
A catalogue record for this book is available from the British
Library

ISBN 0-9536280-3-5
(First published with ISBN 1-900381-03-6)

Printed and bound by Biddles Ltd.

*Cover Photographs: Paul, Ruzzi and Eve with their mother, Heemstede, 1937
and Bergen-Belsen, 1945*

CONTENTS

Part Four

LIBERATION

Alive but alone

Part Five

AFTER THE WAR

A second life

Part Six

INTO RETIREMENT

Beyond my dreams

EPILOGUE

The birds of Belsen

APPENDICES

MAPS

FOREWORD

Time is running out. Memory will soon become history. Now we can
talk together. Soon, even that luxury will be gone.
As the Holocaust recedes into history, works such as this one become all
the more important. Here, in the story of his own life, Paul
Oppenheimer has shown how the Nazi years almost destroyed one
family. In so doing, he also details its effects on countless millions of
other people.

In 1933, when the Nazis came to power, Paul was a young child
about to start school in Berlin. By the time he was of school leaving
age, he had lived in three different countries, experienced the trauma of
ghettoisation, deportation and incarceration and had lost his parents
and four grandparents to Hitler's genocidal policies.

Paul's story is not as traumatic as others you may encounter. His
family was in a more 'privileged' position, as Jews kept for potential
exchange. But do not be deceived. Paul's dispassionate narrative
sometimes belies the true intensity of the fear, terror and horrific
consequences which accompanied it.

FROM BELSEN TO BUCKINGHAM PALACE

This is an illuminating insight into a period in history, about which we perhaps still know less about than we should. Paul carefully details how the Nazis imposed their will on the Jews through the creeping legislation of the Third Reich and the severe consequences for the Jewish populace. At each step of this process, one senses the terrible dilemma his parents faced; obeying 'the law' on the one hand, while fearing its consequences on the other.

Paul's detailed, careful and accurate account helps us in our understanding of issues so important for our time. It joins many hundreds of other testimonies, each as tragic, each as painful, as the horrors of the camps still unfold. It is to these people that we owe much of what we know and understand of the personal tragedy of the Nazi years.

Holocaust survivor testimonies such as this have not been published to create literary masterpieces, but to tell and to tell again that which needs to be heard and heard again.

Dr. Stephen D. Smith, MBE

ACKNOWLEDGEMENTS

I regret that I was never close enough to my parents really to get to know them before they perished at the early age of 43. They did not keep a diary or record significant events in their lives. I would like to know more about them and why they did and did not take certain courses of action. But it is all too late for that now.

This has prompted me to write my memoirs. In the first instance this is for my family, so that my children and grandchildren will understand my background and what I and my brother and sister went through. At the same time, I would like my contribution to perpetuate the memory of the Holocaust and the tragic involvement of our family in it.

Many members of my family played an important part in my life and I am pleased to recognise and thank all of them. Nevertheless, I should single out a few specific family members, especially those who were a part of my wartime and post-war experiences:

FROM BELSEN TO BUCKINGHAM PALACE

- My parents Hans and Rita, who provided a loving and comfortable home, often under very difficult circumstances.
- My brother Ruzzi, who helped me to survive in the camps and who remembers much more than I do.
- My sister Eve, born in Britain, an important fact that saved us from the gas chambers.
- My uncle and aunt, Rudi and Lotte, who looked after Eve, Ruzzi and me, like their own children.
- My wife Corinne, whose loving support and encouragement has always been and always will be invaluable.
- My children Nick, Simon and Judith, whose interest in my story has stimulated my efforts.

I wish to take this opportunity to thank Dr Thomas Rahe at the Belsen Documentation Centre; Jack Santcross, fellow child survivor of Westerbork and Belsen, and Rob Hadley, freelance photographer. They started me off in 1990 towards remembering my experiences of the Holocaust and telling my story to adult groups, college students and schoolchildren.

During one of my talks in 1994, I met Stephen Smith, who has supported and encouraged my Holocaust activities ever since. Stephen and his remarkable family created Beth Shalom, the first Holocaust Education Centre in Britain. His devotion to the education of schoolchildren and young adults about the Holocaust, coupled with his amazing drive and energy, have inspired me to write this book. I wish to recognise the invaluable assistance of Stephen Smith and his family at Beth Shalom, to which I donate all my royalties.

I have researched the background information for this book to the best of my ability. I apologise in advance for any inadvertent errors.

Paul Oppenheimer, Solihull 1996

DEDICATION

To our first grandson,
Alexander

In memory
of my parents

INTRODUCTION

"Sir, how did you manage to remember all this?" asked a 12-year-old girl, after I had told my story to 250 children at a secondary school in Hampshire. What a good question. I had never faced this one before, but it offered the opportunity for some important explanations.

Obviously, I do not remember everything that happened to me more than 50 years ago. I was 16 years old when World War II ended, and I have had to assemble my story from a variety of sources.

Firstly, I have always remembered most of the major milestones of my life story; for example, that I was born in Berlin, that we lived in Neu-Tempelhof, that I attended a state school in Berlin, and so on. I also remember basic facts about all the places where we lived before and during the war. Furthermore, there are many events which are forever imprinted in my mind, such as the German invasion of Holland on 10 May 1940, the attack by Allied planes on our train in April 1945, and the chance meeting with our sister, Eve, in Leipzig after our liberation.

Secondly, when I first tried to recall my experiences of the Holocaust for a book about survivors and refugees in Birmingham (by Zoë Josephs) during the 1980s, I did so together with my younger brother Rudi (known within our family as 'Ruzzi', pronounced 'Rutsi'). He is three years younger than me, but surprisingly, he remembered much more detail than I did in our conversations. But we also tended to stimulate each other towards remembering events which, until then, we had both forgotten. There were many incidents that had totally slipped my memory, but when Ruzzi mentioned them, it all came back to me quite clearly. There are many examples, especially relating to our time in Westerbork and Bergen-Belsen, when Ruzzi remembered names, the food, the hostage exchanges, or life on the train – I only remembered the lice!

Thirdly, I was extremely fortunate to possess many documents and photographs with which I have confirmed and elaborated my story. For example, I still own two of my yellow stars which I wore for three years during the war. I have kept my *Badekarte* (bath card) and *Arbeitskarte* (work card) from Westerbork, and my Displaced Persons Registration Record from the Allied Expeditionary Force in Maastricht. In addition, my parents passed many of our possessions, documents and photographs to non-Jewish friends in Holland for safe-keeping. We retrieved most of these invaluable items after the war. My school reports, diplomas, certificates, and dozens of pre-war family photographs are all now back in my possession. We also recovered some of the postcards and letters which my parents wrote from Westerbork to their non-Jewish friends in Amsterdam. These documents have all proved most helpful in confirming many facts and dates.

Lastly, I have visited Belsen, Yad Vashem and other Holocaust museums; I have read many books on the Holocaust, and especially books by survivors of Westerbork and Belsen;[1] I have listened to historians lecturing about the Holocaust, and I have talked to fellow survivors at the Hendon Survivors' Centre and elsewhere. This accumulated knowledge does not necessarily alter what I have to say about my personal story, but it has assisted my understanding of the context of my experience.

These factors have not only stimulated me towards remembering many events that both Ruzzi and I had forgotten, but I also discovered many related facts which we never knew during the war, but which are an important part of my story. In Westerbork for example, there were weekly transports 'for re-settlement in the east', but it was only after the war that I found out that these transports went to Auschwitz and Sobibor, and found out what happened to most of the deportees, including my four grandparents. Similarly, I have gleaned much pertinent detail about Bergen-Belsen from the book by Prof. Eberhard Kolb, and about the Nazi occupation of Holland from the documents collected by the *Joods Historisch Museum* in Amsterdam. I hope that the addition of such factual information will enhance my story and provide the reader with a better background of the prevailing conditions in Holland and in Germany, before and during the war.

There are already many memoirs about the Holocaust, including those written by camp survivors, and there are many similarities in all the stories. I believe this to be constructive, as it helps confirm the evidence of what really happened in those dark and distant days. Each survivor has also experienced some special and unique events and occasions, which make every story different, and worth the telling. In my case, I had a younger sister,

---

[1] The camp was called Bergen-Belsen. After liberation by the British Army in 1945, it became known as 'Belsen'.

Eve, who was born in London. This may not seem particularly novel, but during the war, in Holland under German occupation, it was rare indeed and eventually saved my life. There were very few British Jews in the concentration camps. Because of her British citizenship, we were classified as 'exchange' Jews and we were 'privileged' to be sent to the *Sternlager* (Star Camp) in Bergen-Belsen. This forms the basis of my story, and that of my brother Ruzzi and sister Eve.

Sometimes fact is stranger than fiction, but this is not a novel, this is a true story of my experiences before, during and after the war. I have therefore endeavoured to present an accurate account to the best of my knowledge. Unfortunately, I cannot present my experiences as eloquently as Anne Frank, Elie Wiesel or Richard Dimbleby, because I am a scientist and professional engineer, used to dealing with facts and figures and not trained to describe feelings and emotions. I can only do it my way, and I hope that it will add something to our knowledge and understanding of that terrible period in history which we have come to call the Holocaust.

PART ONE

BUCKINGHAM PALACE TO BELSEN

A journey through time

Photo: Paul Oppenheimer

A VERY IMPORTANT LETTER

Solihull. November 1989.

Armistice Day, 1989. It was the morning of the 11th day of the 11th month, when the letter dropped through our letterbox. It was a cream envelope, imprinted with:

'*On Her Majesty's Service.*

'*URGENT*

'*PERSONAL*

'*PRIME MINISTER*'

"This must be for you, Corinne," I suggested to my wife. "No, it is addressed to P. Oppenheimer Esq.," she replied. "What have I done now?" I wondered, and gingerly opened the envelope with care and curiosity. The letter was from 10 Downing Street. It stated 'IN CONFIDENCE' at the top of the page.

'The Prime Minister ... has it in mind ... to submit your name to the Queen ... to approve that you be appointed a Member of the Order of the British Empire.'

FROM BELSEN TO BUCKINGHAM PALACE

I could not believe what I was reading. I read on.

'The Prime Minister would be glad to be assured that this would be agreeable to you.'

I showed the letter to Corinne and when I had recovered from the shock, completed the enclosed reply form and confirmed that I was indeed agreeable to the Prime Minister's recommendation that I be awarded the MBE.

It was in strict confidence and I was not to tell anybody about this award before the New Year Honours List was published, not *even* our three children – *especially* not our three children. Of course, Corinne had seen the letter, but we really told nobody else about it, for the next seven weeks. It was difficult at first, but then I forgot about it, except that I sometimes wondered why I should be honoured and for what? The letter did not mention this, but added,

'You will receive no further communication before the List is published.'

They were right. Absolutely nothing happened until Friday 29 December 1989, when various press reporters, who had previewed the honours list, telephoned and started asking questions. That was the first confirmation that I had really been honoured with the MBE.

The next day, Saturday 30 December 1989, the New Year Honours List was published in all the major newspapers. There were photographs of politicians David Steel, William Waldegrave and John Patten, industrialists Trevor Chinn and George Turnbull, actress Maggie Smith, and sports personalities Frank Bruno, Sebastian Coe, Tony Jacklin and Bryan Robson. There was also my name in the *Financial Times* list: 'Mr Paul Oppenheimer, regulations and standards manager, Lucas Automotive'. There

A VERY IMPORTANT LETTER

was a bit more in the *Birmingham Post, Evening Mail* and *Express &
Star*: '... aged 61, from Dorridge'.

I still did not know who had submitted my name and why. It
seemed pretty obvious that the award was for my work on
international road vehicle safety standards and regulations for the
motor industry in Brussels (European Union) and in Geneva
(United Nations). I assumed that my colleagues in the UK
Department of Transport had nominated me. Later I found out
that they had intended to nominate me, but had forgotten to do so,
and it was probably the management at my employers, Lucas
Automotive Ltd, that had put my name forward. It is a question
that I should have asked at the time, but I was too embarrassed.

The following week, letters started to arrive from friends and
colleagues, and from people I had never even heard of – but it was
very nice of them to write all the same! Letters came from the
local Lord Lieutenant representing Her Majesty The Queen; the
Permanent Secretary of the Department of Trade and Industry; the
Chairman of Lucas Industries; the Mayor of Solihull; colleagues
within the motor industry, the local community and our
synagogue.

A few days later, the local reporters from the *Solihull News* and
the *Solihull Times* came to our house. It only took six questions:
"How old are you? How long have you lived here in Solihull?
Where did you live before? Where were you born? When did you
come to England? Where were you during the war?" As soon as I
mentioned that I had been in Belsen during the war, the journalists
wanted to know all about the camp and they soon forgot about the
medal. 'MBE for Belsen survivor' was the headline in the next
issue.

FROM BELSEN TO BUCKINGHAM PALACE

One of the photographers was Rob Hadley, a war buff in touch with the Imperial War Museum. He told me that there would be a special reunion in Belsen during April that year (1990), to commemorate the 45th Anniversary of the liberation of Belsen and to celebrate the inauguration of a new documentation centre there. He asked me whether I would like to attend, and after some consultations with my family, we decided to go. Together with the press photographer and a reporter from the *Solihull Times*, my younger brother Ruzzi (who had shared all my wartime experiences and who lived in Holland at that time), my daughter Judith (aged 19 and very much interested in her Judaism and the Holocaust), I went on a journey to Belsen, which for the second time was about to change my life....

RETURN TO BELSEN
Anniversary of the Liberation. April 1990.

Yom Ha Shoah – the annual Jewish 'Day of the Holocaust' – seemed an appropriate day on which to revisit Belsen, the site of the infamous German concentration camp during World War II. It was 45 years after the liberation of the camp by the British Army in April 1945, and it coincided with the opening of a new documentation centre at the Belsen *Gedenkstätte* (Memorial Site) on 22 April 1990. An official programme of events had been arranged to commemorate the anniversary.

I had been back to Belsen in 1953 and in 1987, and therefore knew what to expect. There is nothing left of the original concentration camp. There are no barracks or fences, no guard towers, no barbed wire, no dirt, no mud and no smell of death. They have all disappeared. Everything was totally burned and destroyed by the British to prevent the spread of disease and infection in May 1945. The only recognisable feature today is the railway siding, no more than a few miles from the camp, where we arrived in the winter of 1944. It is interesting that this railway siding is within one mile of the town of Bergen, whose inhabitants claimed to know nothing about the camp during the war.

The original entrance to the camp can still be recognised, by a clear avenue through the tall pine trees, leading from the camp towards the railway tracks. It is said that no trees or bushes can grow on this path, trodden by thousands and thousands of prisoners. Perhaps it has just been left uncultivated as a mark of respect for them. The only features to remind us of the past are the mass graves – huge mounds of earth covered in grass, concealing thousands of dead bodies. Almost 50,000 victims, mostly Jews, perished here in Belsen.

Today, the Memorial site is approximately half a mile square, a flat and desolate clearing surrounded by pine woods, and covered by heather as part of the surrounding *Lüneburgerheide* (Lüneburg Heath). There is an eerie calm, and there appear to be few animals, although Judith found a yellow butterfly. The principal sound today is still the thunder of British tanks and artillery in the nearby military training area of Hohne.

On this day the guns were quiet for our return. It was 45 years since I had been here during World War II. It started me thinking, and when we met the other survivors during the subsequent reunion in the evening, the memories of our wartime experiences came flooding back ... and it all still seemed so vivid....

BEFORE THE WAR

Memories from childhood

Photo: Mother, Ruzzi, Eve and I. Heemstede, 1937

AT HOME WITH THE ENEMY
Berlin, September 1928 – March 1936

My father, Johann (Hans) Felix Robert Oppenheimer, was born in Fürth near Nuremberg in Germany on 18 June 1901. My mother Friederike (Rita) Fürst was born in Heidelberg on 23 January 1902. They were both Jewish and they met at Heidelberg University where both gained doctorates in philosophy. I still possess my father's original typed manuscript of his thesis – *The logic of the sociological concept formation with special reference to Max Weber* – and the first prize gold medal which was awarded to him by the University for this thesis. In the 750th Anniversary commemoration book of the town of Oppenheim, his name is mentioned alongside those of Harry Oppenheimer, the diamond millionaire (no relation) and Robert Oppenheimer, father of the atomic bomb (also no relation). I also have my mother's PhD certificate, granted in June 1928, for her thesis on *August Ludwig von Schlözer, a German enlightener in the 18th Century.*

FROM BELSEN TO BUCKINGHAM PALACE

My father did not pursue his academic career and entered the world of commerce for financial reasons. In 1925/26, he worked for 12 months in the Berlin Chamber of Commerce. He was described as talented, thorough and hard-working, by the president of the Chamber, Franz von Mendelssohn. He was promptly offered a job as a commercial counsellor in the family bank, Mendelssohn & Company in Berlin. He was offered a very attractive salary, which he could not refuse.

In 1927, my father married Rita Fürst, his sweetheart colleague from Heidelberg University, and they settled in the Neu-Tempelhof area of Berlin to raise a family. I do not recall that my mother went out to work.

At that time, Berlin was the capital city of Germany and a world-renowned cultural and intellectual centre with excellent public transport, shopping areas, and many parks and lakes for recreation and amusement. The German population comprised over 500,000 Jews. A third of these lived in Berlin, which was one of the largest and most flourishing Jewish communities in Europe. A quarter of the Jews living in Berlin were foreigners, most of whom originated from Poland, Russia and Austria. They tended to live together in the eastern parts of the city, while most German Jews lived in the centre of Berlin and in the affluent areas of Charlottenburg, Tiergarten and Schöneberg. Many German Jews were proudly patriotic and appear to have lived relatively isolated from the organised Jewish Community. They identified more with the German people, thus making them less conscious of their Jewish identity – at least in the beginning, before the rise to power of Adolf Hitler.

I believe that my parents endeavoured to live like good Germans, with respect for authority and the law. I have certainly inherited some of my parents' German characteristics, such as a sense of order, discipline, and attention to detail, which have proved useful in my later life. Apparently, German Jews did not often show their feelings and were not anxious, even among themselves, to be seen as distinctly Jewish.

I was born on 20 September 1928 in a nursing home in the Berlin district of Charlottenburg. According to my birth certificate, I was named Paul Friedrich Oppenheimer, although I dropped the Germanic 'Friedrich' at a convenient opportunity in 1945. Our home was at 3 Zähringer Korso in Neu-Tempelhof, very close to Tempelhof airport – one of the first airports in Europe, and still in operation today. Three years later, on 1 October 1931, my brother Rudolf (Ruzzi) was born, and the two of us experienced most of the events of the next 15 years (before and during the war) together. I understand that we were a respectable, middle-class family. We called our parents Vali and Muli. We also had a non-Jewish nanny called Jula (from my grandparents in Heidelberg), who stayed with us during our early years in Berlin.

We lived in a traditional German house, with three storeys and a cellar. We also had a balcony to sit on in the sun, but no garage as few people owned cars in Berlin when our house was built in the 1920s. There were three or four bedrooms and a nice garden for us to enjoy. We have many photographs, showing us playing in the back garden and in our sandpit. The sandpit is where Ruzzi got the first of his three head injuries in 1936, when I accidentally pushed him out of the sandpit.

The S-Bahn tram passed near our house. This was our principal form of transport. We possessed no car and no bicycles in Berlin. We watched the occasional test-flying and aerobatic demonstrations above the Tempelhof airport from our garden –

Herr Udet was the star performer in those days – and we regularly watched the huge Zeppelin airships fly overhead on their way to and from Tempelhof. At the weekends we visited Grunewald Park, the Berlin Zoo and many other attractions. Our photographs at the zoo, in our matching beige woolly suits and hats, remind us of our happy days in Berlin. My father was a train-spotter and we often walked to the Anhalter Bahnhof to see the fascinating colourful international trains, destined to travel all over Europe. These were some of the few precious moments that I enjoyed with my father. Among our birthday presents in 1935 was a Märklin (00 gauge) table-top electric train set, which we have back in our possession today. We visited our grandparents in Nuremberg and Heidelberg. I also remember studying Baedeker guide books before our summer holidays in Baden-Baden in the Black Forest, Marienbad in Czechoslovakia and Seelisberg above the Vierwaldstätter See, in Switzerland. We had visits from my father's younger brother Rudi and sister Liesl, who later emigrated to England and Palestine, respectively. I loved my parents and family, but I especially admired Uncle Rudi. He was more than six feet tall and looked strong and fit, usually walking around the house and garden in his university football shorts. He was very much a sportsman, rather than an academic scholar like my father. Obviously, my parents also admired Uncle Rudi, because my brother (Rudolf) and I (Paul Friedrich) were both named after my uncle (Friedrich Rudolf Oppenheimer).

I started school in 1935 and attended a local state school. I still have the end-of-term reports from the No.3 *Volksschule*, showing a grade one for German language and mathematics. I also have a class photograph from this school in Berlin, with a picture of Adolf Hitler at the back of the classroom. I was probably the only Jewish child in the class. I sometimes wonder what happened to all the other classmates and how many of them are alive today. I have another photograph, taken on my first day at school, with two German friends, carrying the traditional large cone of sweets and chocolates. Amongst the variety of documents in our possession now, I was surprised to find a report confirming that I also attended the Religion School of the Jewish Community in Berlin during 1935, presumably on Sunday mornings. However, I remember nothing about any early Jewish religious activities at home. I believe that we were quite assimilated, like many German Jews at that time.

To my knowledge very few Jewish families lived in Neu-Tempelhof. We were Jewish, but not religious. My parents seemed to enjoy their early life in Berlin, despite the difficult times of unemployment and inflation, and of course the stirrings of antisemitism.

The cause of the rise of National Socialism pre-dated my birth, to the time of the First World War and its aftermath. The restrictions placed on Germany through the Versailles Treaty, and the subsequent political and economic instability through the 1920s, led to a rise in extremist political parties offering radical solutions to Germany's problems.

An interesting example of the disastrous period of hyperinflation is provided by the letters which my father wrote from Heidelberg University to his parents in Nuremberg during 1923. The postage stamps on these letters in my possession increased from a hundred marks in May to a thousand marks in August, five million marks in October and ten thousand million marks in November 1923, and back to ten marks in January 1924. The same was happening to the price of basic commodities. Many

Germans lost most of their financial resources during this period. This was followed by the great depression of 1929, when millions of Germans were unemployed and there were soup kitchens in the streets. This was fertile ground for the ideas of Hitler and the Nazis. The Jews became convenient scapegoats and antisemitism flourished. Many Germans may not have agreed with the Nazi philosophies, but found it expedient to join the Nazi Party.

The Nazis promised jobs for the unemployed who supported the Party, and they kept their word. Thousands were engaged in the preparations for war, working in armament factories, building the first *Autobahnen* (motorways) or joining the military. The Nazis also promised food, holidays and entertainment for the workers. Teenagers were encouraged to join the Hitler Youth. There were additional incentives for men prepared to join the Nazi elite squads, such as the SA (*Sturmabteilung* – Storm Troopers), SD (*Sicherheitsdienst* – Security Service) and SS (*Schutzstaffel* – Protection Squad). On the other hand, many German professionals had the unenviable choice of joining the Nazi Party or losing their jobs. Jews were not wanted in the Nazi Party, Hitler Youth or anywhere else.

Even before Adolf Hitler came to power in 1933, the Nazis began to make life uncomfortable for the Jewish population of Berlin. There were unofficial boycotts and attacks on Jewish shops with worrying frequency. But in 1933, when Hitler was appointed *Reichskanzler* (Chancellor) of Germany, the official government-sponsored persecution of the Jews intensified almost immediately. Decrees were issued week by week and month by month, forcing Jews out of their livelihoods, restricting their activities and ultimately isolating them from the German community. Some of the earlier racial laws, promulgated before our departure in 1936, included the following:

- Jewish doctors were not allowed to practise in hospitals;
- Jewish lawyers were not permitted to represent Berlin;
- Jewish judges were dismissed;
- Jewish teachers were dismissed from state schools;
- Jewish officials were dismissed from state service;
- Jews were excluded from sports and gymnastics clubs;
- Jews were not allowed at Wannsee beach (particularly intriguing in view of Wannsee's subsequent notoriety);
- Jews were not allowed to be professional musicians, actors or actresses, art or antique dealers;
- Outings of more than 20 Jewish youths were prohibited;
- Marriages and intercourse between Germans and Jews would be punished – such interfaith marriages were invalid;
- Baptism and transfers to Christian religions were not valid;
- Journalists had to prove their Aryan heritage, and that of their partners, back to 1800.

One of the fundamental set of Nazi laws was published in September 1935: the 'Nuremberg Laws' differentiated between 'citizens' – who must be of pure German blood – and 'subjects'. Citizens and subjects were not permitted to cohabit 'for the protection of German blood and honour'. Furthermore, these laws later went on to clarify who would be considered as a Jew by the Nazi government. This depended primarily on the number of Jewish grandparents an individual had and their affiliation to the Jewish community.

This was the situation until 1936. During the memorable Olympic Games in Berlin in the summer of 1936 all anti-Jewish propaganda was temporarily suspended. This did not mean that antisemitic hatred ceased or that racism did not exist. Jesse Owens, the African American athlete, inferior in the eyes of the Aryan 'master race', won four gold medals to the obvious disgust of Adolf Hitler. After the games, life returned to 'normal' and the proliferation of anti-Jewish laws accelerated. Jews were soon to be virtually excluded from all forms of public life.

I do not remember that we were directly affected at first. In fact, Ruzzi enjoyed the bands marching through the streets and often followed behind with the other children – until my mother explained that these brown-uniformed goose-stepping Storm Troopers, with the swastika armbands and the big jackboots, hated us and we should not associate with them. On the wireless, we heard Hitler addressing the huge Nazi Party rallies, ranting and raving, blaming the Jews for all their misfortunes. This hate-mongering was supported by a most effective state propaganda machine on the wireless, in the newspapers and especially on the streets. There were anti-Jewish posters and slogans in city streets and later on shop windows and public buildings.

I have been asked how we reacted to all this anti-Jewish propaganda and activity. I was only four years old when Hitler came to power and I was not really aware of any difficulties. I cannot remember that we were ever physically attacked, either at school or in the streets, or that we were otherwise ostracised in Berlin. Anyway, most of the earlier anti-Jewish laws did not directly affect us. Apart from the marching bands, there would be gangs of Nazis roaming the streets and attacking Jews and their property, but this did not seem to happen in our area. Of course, there was no television in those days and I did not read the newspapers at that age. When I encountered all these anti-Jewish laws again five years later in Holland, under German occupation, I was more aware of the situation and better able to express my reactions. But no doubt my parents must have been most apprehensive and worried about our future in Germany. More and more Jewish families were leaving Germany in a bloodless pogrom, even before 1933, and in increasing numbers after 1933. The day in May 1933 when the Nazis systematically burned all 'Jewish' books on bonfires in the streets must have frightened my parents enormously. But even emigration was becoming difficult, as the Nazis prohibited Jews from taking their possessions abroad with them. Another, even bigger obstacle to this emigration was the erection of barriers to immigration in many other countries, either by the imposition of entry quotas or by other procedures. In general, Jewish refugees were not finding a welcome anywhere.

Our parents never discussed their fears or plans with Ruzzi or me, but they must have spent many anxious hours urgently debating what to do for the best for their family. Did they share the eternal liberal optimism of some of the German Jews at that time, or were they able to foresee the elimination of the Jews from the Third Reich, as promised by Adolf Hitler in his noisy speeches and in his manifesto, *Mein Kampf*? As the persecution of the Jews in Germany accelerated, they must have deliberated long and hard on the few remaining options. Eventually, after corresponding with Uncle Rudi in London, they made up their minds and decided to take action and to leave Germany. Their fateful decision is recorded in my father's postcard from Berlin to his brother in London, dated 24 March 1936 (see Appendix 3).

My mother: Friederike (Rita)
Oppenheimer née Fürst

My father: Johann (Hans) Felix Robert
Oppenheimer

Ruzzi and I at the Berlin Zoo, 1934

Ruzzi and I with Uncle Rudi, 1934

Mother and I, 1931.

My first day at school with two German classmates, 1935

In class in Berlin, 1935.
The picture on the classroom wall (top right) was of Adolf Hitler;
my own children scratched it off the original.

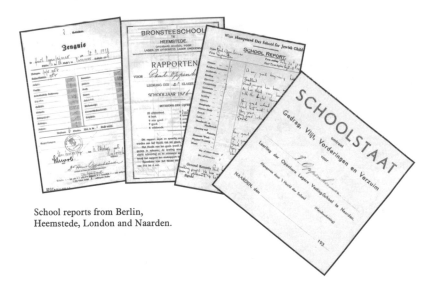

School reports from Berlin,
Heemstede, London and Naarden.

Part of a series of nine letters sent by
my father to his father in 1923,
clearly indicating the problem of
inflation Germany was experiencing
at the time.

21 May
100 Marks

12 August
1,000 Marks

26 September
250,000 Marks

16 November
10,000,000,000 Marks

BORN IN BRITAIN

London. March 1936 – September 1936.

On 24 March, 1936, Mother, Ruzzi and I left Berlin, with the limited possessions that we could carry in our suitcases. We travelled by train to Ostend in Belgium and from there to Dover, and on to Uncle Rudi and Aunt Lotte in London. Father remained behind in Berlin. In Ostend, Ruzzi sustained his second head injury, as I pulled him along in order not to miss the ferry. My mother was six months pregnant at this time and this may have had something to do with the timing of our journey. I have never found out why my father did not come with us to seek sanctuary in England. My understanding has always been that he could not get an entry visa or a work permit or suitable employment, but there may have been other reasons. Apparently there was a British policy of 'no admission without financial guarantees' at some time during this era and my father may have fallen foul of this demand.

FROM BELSEN TO BUCKINGHAM PALACE

In retrospect, it was obviously tragic that he did not accompany us to England, but it did not seem very important *why* he did not come with us – and I never asked my parents such questions, either then or later. Our trip to England was described to Ruzzi and me as a 'holiday'. This did not seem right, since we started to go to school in London almost as soon as we arrived. Furthermore, we were sure that we would not be going back to Berlin at the end of our 'holiday'. But many other Jewish families were leaving Germany *en masse* at that time and even later. Why we did not escape as a family remains a mystery to this day.

Perhaps we got out of Germany just in time. After the Evian Conference in July 1938, convened by President Roosevelt to address the plight of 'involuntary refugees', and the infamous *Kristallnacht* in November of the same year, the Nazi oppression of the Jews intensified further. The United States and Britain maintained their quota system and refused to absorb additional numbers of Jews. Most of the few Jewish refugees that were subsequently allowed into Britain were children, notably the *Kindertransports* (children's transports), which brought some 10,000 Jewish children to Britain – but sadly, without their parents.

I was seven years old when I arrived in England and was delighted to be staying with Uncle Rudi again. We lived in London with him and his wife Lotte in their apartment at 30 The Avenue, in Kilburn in northwest London, which was a popular area for Jewish refugees from Germany, especially for academics and professional people. Uncle Rudi and Aunt Lotte had emigrated from Germany in 1934 and married in London later in the same year. They had both qualified as lawyers in Germany, but were unable to practise law in England, not only because English and German law were based on different principles, but also because it was difficult for refugees to enter the legal profession in England. Like many other refugees from the Continent, they were forced to abandon their chosen professional careers, disregard their many years of study and training, and go out to find alternative employment.

Uncle Rudi established himself in the 'rag' trade and soon became a respected member of this growing community. He loved life in England for the tolerance and personal freedom, and also for the importance of sports in everyday life. He had been an excellent football player and swimmer in Germany, competing for his university. I admired his photographs of himself in goal for the football team and doing swallow-dives from the highest Olympic diving boards. Uncle Rudi was an early role model for me and I later learned to play and appreciate many different sports, including football and swimming. He was also a car enthusiast and proud owner of a bullnose Morris Cowley, which he sold for £5 to Stewart & Arden in Berkeley Square. His exploits involved the buying and selling of various other second-hand cars (Singer, Lea Francis, Wolseley, etc.) for sums of up to £10, and regular discussions with police officers who seemed to know and appreciate his extrovert motoring habits. Uncle Rudi was an ardent stamp collector, which became another bond between us. Later in life, he specialised in stamps from the state of Bavaria and developed a unique collection of stamps, envelopes and postal history. He was also a talented player of his grand piano and enjoyed hammering Wagner at all hours of the day and night – to the disgust of Lotte and to the dismay of the neighbours.

I enjoyed our stay with Uncle Rudi and Aunt Lotte, who was an excellent cook, with recipes for many tasty German dishes. I particularly remember visiting the Whipsnade Zoo, a huge open-air parkland where the animals roamed around – so very different from Berlin, and most other zoos at that time. Ruzzi and I went to school at the West Hampstead Day School for Jewish children in Willesden Lane and we soon learned to speak some English. I was very excited that I was allowed to wear long trousers to school for the first time in my life, and rather earlier than would be allowed on the Continent – I felt very grown up at the age of seven. We played in the street and I was particularly impressed with the local trolley buses. We often visited friends of Uncle Rudi and Aunt Lotte, mostly refugees from Germany. One of them lived in a house called 'Sholem' in Hampstead Heath, which had a small swimming pool in the back garden and there Ruzzi suffered his third head injury. I cannot remember whether I had anything to do with it this time, but we have a photograph to record the bandaged result.

The most important event during our stay in England was the birth of my sister, Rachel Eve Dorothy, on 23 June 1936. Born in Hendon, she had a British birth certificate and as such was classed as a British subject. We did not realise at this stage just how significant this simple fact would eventually turn out to be. Whether this was just a fortunate coincidence, or whether my parents had foreseen the significance of British citizenship already in 1936, is another question that I failed to ask earlier in my life. Obviously my mother was already pregnant when we left Berlin, and maybe my parents just expected better hospital treatment for a Jewish mother in London than in Berlin.

Soon after the birth of Eve, my father, who had remained in Germany, found employment in the Amsterdam branch of the Mendelssohn Bank. He left Berlin to settle in Heemstede, a small town about 15 miles west of Amsterdam. On 20 September 1936, my eighth birthday, we left London to join my father in Holland, where he would see his baby daughter, Eve, for the first time. With hindsight, our return to continental Europe was a tragic mistake. Perhaps there were few other options for our family if we wanted to live together. There was also the hopeful expectation that Holland would keep out of any forthcoming war between Germany and Britain.

OUT OF HARM'S WAY

Heemstede. September 1936 – October 1940.

Heemstede is a minor suburb of Haarlem and only a few miles from the Dutch seaside resort of Zandvoort. We lived in a nice new semi-detached house at number 11, Johannes Vermeer Straat, in a rural and pleasant area of Heemstede. It was very quiet compared to London and Berlin. To start with, none of us could speak any Dutch although we tried to speak it at home, which proved to be easier for the children than the parents. My father preferred to speak German throughout our stay in Holland and in the camps. My mother, on the other hand, picked up Dutch during her meetings with neighbours and at the shops. We children had no problem adapting to another new language and spoke Dutch all day at school and with our new Dutch friends.

My father had managed to bring some of our property and personal possessions from Berlin, including his upright Steinway piano, but he may have been forced to abandon some of his financial assets, including our house in Berlin. We were noticeably less affluent in Holland than we were in Berlin. For example, we had no more holidays in Switzerland. I was not old enough or inquisitive enough to enquire about such things.

There was a tram from Zandvoort to Amsterdam which my father used daily to go to the office. The rest of us went everywhere by foot or by bicycle. Another German Jewish refugee family called Mainz, with two daughters our age, Eva and Marianne, happened to live across the road from us. Generally however, there were few Jews in this part of Holland. There was a synagogue in nearby Haarlem, but I cannot recall ever attending services there. We did, however, have a blue-and-white Jewish National Fund collection box in our front room in Heemstede – perhaps in recognition of our Aunt Liesl, my father's younger sister, who had emigrated to Palestine. My father succeeded in getting all our four grandparents out of Germany. My father's parents Josef and Meta (*née* Baum) from Nuremberg and my mother's parents Dr Rudolf and Hedwig (*née* Oppé) Fürst from Heidelberg lived together in a small house not far from us in Heemstede. We lived a very ordinary and mundane life in Heemstede, yet these were some of the best years of my life.

I started school immediately and had to learn Dutch – my third school language – in 1936. Fortunately, Dutch is a language (or is it a throat disease?) with links to German and English, and as I was immersed in Dutch all day I picked it up very quickly. I also learned Dutch geography and history for four years. Holland was another seagoing country, like Britain, with a substantial number of colonies in the East and West Indies, and I had to learn all about Java, Sumatra, Borneo, Curaçao, Guyana and Surinam. The Dutch had often been in conflict with Spain and England. It was interesting to note, in my classes, that the Dutch version of the history of the Royal House of Orange and the related wars and battles was somewhat different from the English version!

I learned woodworking and produced a fine model of the Dutch Royal Family crest, which we have on display today at home. After two years at the Bronstee School, I transferred in 1938 to the new Craijenester School, also in Heemstede, and stayed there for another two years. I still have all the relevant school reports. The only subject in which I ever had poor marks was singing!

One of my best classmates, Jürgen Comello, was from an immigrant family from Surinam. I went to visit him a couple of years ago. Amazingly, he still lives at the same address in Haarlem 60 years later. There was a 50th Anniversary reunion of my class in 1989. Unfortunately, I missed it because they could not find me, but I heard about it during a visit in 1990, when I met three of my erstwhile classmates; Jürgen Comello, Jan ten Hagen, and Ab Slendebroek.

These were some of the best times of my childhood and I have cherished memories of those years in Heemstede. I really enjoyed going to school and I had many friends at school and in our street. I played football and went swimming, almost daily, and there was lots of cycling. We were the proud possessors of a *Vliegende Holländer* (Flying Dutchman) which was like a soap box on four wheels. It did not move as fast as a bicycle, but it provided an exciting ride nevertheless. Swimming was almost compulsory in Holland, because of the many canals, rivers and lakes. After school we went to the indoor pool in Haarlem or, in the summer, the outdoor pool in Aerdenhout. On two occasions I finished up in hospital: playing football around the side of the pool and falling through the reinforced glass screens, and falling off the high diving board onto the ceramic tiles. But I suppose this was all part of the fun.

These were also our best years with our parents at home. Unfortunately, we never really got to know them well enough to describe their inner feelings and emotions, their likes and dislikes or what made them tick. We only remember their superficial features. My father was short and stocky, with a round face and spectacles; he was always meticulously dressed in a dark three-piece suit. I cannot remember ever seeing him in a sports jacket, shorts, or wearing a sweater. My mother was a fabulous knitter. She spent hours and hours knitting all sorts of clothing, especially for Eve.

In 1937, the International Boy Scout Jamboree was held in Vogelenzang, a small village better known for its tulip bulb fields and only a few miles from Heemstede. There were thousands of teenage boys from all over the world and it was fascinating for us local kids to wander through the camp site, visit their tents and exchange souvenirs, like coins, badges, stamps, etc. Lord Baden-Powell was in charge and we attended some of the special ceremonies. Apparently almost every country in the world was represented – except Germany, where the Boy Scouts had been outlawed and replaced with the 'Hitler Youth', who were not welcome.

I recently recovered a few of my diplomas for swimming, including 25 metres fully clothed, a cycling proficiency certificate, a gymnastics diploma and also a local football club membership card. I had played some cricket in Haarlem too.

My father had also developed the philately bug, like Uncle Rudi, and we started collecting stamps from all over the world.

OUT OF HARM'S WAY

Later, we would concentrate on pre-war Germany, Holland and Britain. My father was still a devoted train spotter and we used to go for long walks down to the level crossing by Heemstede's railway station, at the appropriate time in the evening, to watch in fascination while the Blue Train and other major international trains passed, on their way to and from Amsterdam.

At the weekends, we cycled with mother to Zandvoort or to the nearby tulip fields, or we went sightseeing with father, often by tram to Amsterdam, where he enjoyed various specific dishes at his favourite restaurants. We had some fabulous ice-cream delicacies. I do not remember any holidays in Holland, as we probably could not afford such luxuries any more. But we had school outings to a local zoo where my finger was bitten by a monkey, and to the airport at Waalhaven near Rotterdam from which I still have the class photograph.

During the winters, the numerous canals, rivers and lakes in our neighbourhood would freeze over and there was lots of ice-skating, using the strange Dutch wooden skates with steel blades, strapped to our shoes. One day, I went all the way to school on ice skates. It was a long way round on the various canals and the Spaarne river in Haarlem, but great fun. Life was wonderful and there were no restrictions whatsoever. Unfortunately, this carefree and happy life was suddenly and savagely interrupted.

Everything changed on 10 May 1940, the day the Germans invaded Holland, Belgium and France, without warning. It was a complete surprise to all of us and a day that I shall always remember; perhaps the most crucial and significant day of our lives.

The morning sky was clear, blue, and beautiful. There were announcements on the radio about the German invasion and there was lots of noise in the streets. We should have been frightened, but I remember that we were immensely excited. I was 11 years old, and it seemed like a real life adventure story. We could see many planes, high up in the sky with hundreds of white parachutes gliding down over the Dutch countryside. German paratroopers were jumping from the transport planes and landing not far away from us. We also watched the Dutch Army setting up roadblocks to catch German saboteurs and infiltrators in civilian clothing. Everyone coming along the roads was stopped and they had to pronounce the names of various Dutch towns and cities such as Scheveningen, Ymuiden, Groningen, Leeuwarden. No German could get the pronunciation and intonation right, and that is how many German infiltrators were caught. Together with other school friends, we watched in amazement and actually enjoyed the events. I later found out that the Dutch Army had flooded large areas of Holland in order to delay the German invaders, but the paratroopers were landing behind these flooded lines, thus creating total havoc in the Dutch Army. Furthermore, hundreds of ordinary German men and women had entered Holland prior to the invasion and adopted various disguises as clergy, academics, tourists and even as nuns and orthodox Jews. They had infiltrated the Dutch community and were involved in stealing military secrets and making preparations for the invasion. On 10 May, this 'Fifth Column' of guerrillas and saboteurs went into action, to guide and support the invading German troops and to sabotage Dutch railways and military installations. Hence the roadblocks that we had witnessed.

There was also a Nazi Party in Holland – the National Socialist Movement (NSB). However, this was a small organisation of 27,000 members and most Dutch people had ignored their activities. Their leader was Anton Mussert. His adherents wore all-black uniforms and saluted with raised right arms, just like the German Nazis. They emerged on 10 May 1940 and welcomed the German invaders and offered assistance to the German Army. Subsequently, they co-operated with the Nazis and often helped to find and arrest Jews. At a later stage, they were offered a small reward for information leading to the arrest of hidden Jews.

After only five days of this German blitzkrieg, including the wanton bombing of Rotterdam and the threat to flatten the beautiful old city of Amsterdam, the Dutch forces surrendered. They capitulated and we were once more trapped in the Third Reich. We had expected Holland to remain neutral as in World War I. We had hoped that we could have survived peacefully in Holland, until Germany and Britain had settled their differences, but it was not to be.

The Germans wasted no time in occupying Holland and installing Dr Seyss-Inquart as *Reichskommissar* (Reich Commissioner) in supreme control of the government and civic affairs. There was a brief period of calm for the Dutch population to adapt to the new situation. Within six months however, the persecution of the Jews in Holland started, with the gradual introduction of the established anti-Jewish laws from Germany, and our life changed dramatically. We were almost immediately affected, because Jews were not allowed to live in, or visit, the protected areas near the Dutch seaside, where the Germans started to build their military fortifications to repel eventual British landings. And so we had to leave Heemstede, quite suddenly and quickly, after four of the happiest years of my life. On 7 October 1940 we moved to Naarden, just east of Amsterdam and near to the well-known Dutch radio station in Hilversum. We were allowed to take all of our possessions with us to Naarden, where our new home was of similar size to our home in Heemstede.

PART THREE

DURING THE WAR

Life under the Nazis

Photo: The yellow star I wore throughout the war

CALM BEFORE THE STORM
Naarden. October 1940 – May 1942.

Naarden was an old medieval fortress town with a surrounding moat, which was excellent for skating and ice hockey in the winter. We lived on the Huizerstraatweg, just outside the moat, but went to school in the Vesting School inside the fortress. My father continued to work at the bank in Amsterdam, while mother stayed at home. My first memory of Jewish religious activities at home was when my mother invited other local Jewish children for impromptu classes at our house. Obviously my mother knew more about Judaism than I had suspected, and it was the common bond of persecution that started to bring the Jewish families together. We began to attend synagogue services in nearby Bussum. In Berlin, London and Heemstede, I cannot remember ever attending a synagogue service and I had never consciously mixed with other Jewish children, except at school in London, although some of my friends in Heemstede happened to be Jewish. I was 12 years old in

FROM BELSEN TO BUCKINGHAM PALACE

Naarden and it was high time for me to receive some serious Jewish education, if I was to meet my *Bar Mitzvah* obligations in 1941. I could remember little from my Sunday school in Berlin and the Jewish day school in London.

For one reason and another, I never completed my *Bar Mitzvah* on my 13th birthday in September 1941. I did, however, manage to continue my sporting activities in Naarden. There was an indoor swimming pool at the end of our road, and I played football for a local junior team. These were proper matches with an official referee, against teams from other towns and villages, and I remember on one occasion scoring a brilliant winning goal! In the winter we skated on the moat, almost outside our house.

In June 1941 I sat the entrance examinations for the Gooise HBS in Bussum – the local secondary grammar school – and passed with flying colours. Unfortunately, I was unable to complete more than one term at my new school because Jewish children were no longer permitted to attend non-Jewish schools.

My father made many good friends during our time in Naarden, including Richard Haas and his family in Hilversum, who were refugees from Germany but managed to avoid classification as Jews.

We seemed to be living a very normal life, yet all over Holland new laws were being promulgated which were to have a devastating effect on the Jewish community. I am not sure even now whether it was because we were in a relatively small town with relatively few Jewish families, but at this time I was largely unaware of what was happening elsewhere in Holland. Maybe it was because my parents were particularly good at making life seem normal, or perhaps we were just a little more fortunate than others were at this point in time. However, I know now that a comprehensive range of anti-Jewish laws was being introduced to segregate the Jews of Holland.

During the time we were in Naarden some of the laws which were published included:

October 1940: Declaration of Aryan origin. The 1935 Nuremberg Laws were applied to determine who was a Jew, including those of 'mixed blood'. Jews married to non-Jewish partners could volunteer for permanent sterilisation and thus claim exemption from the race laws.

November 1940: Jewish civil servants were dismissed from posts in government and from public office.

January 1941: Jews had to complete a registration form like all Dutch citizens but their *Persoonsbewijs* (identity card) was stamped with a capital 'J'. German Jewish males and females had to add 'Israel' and 'Sara' respectively to their names. German Jews were stripped of their German citizenship and became 'stateless'. I still have both identity cards of my paternal grandparents. Next to their passport photograph is the large capital 'J', and the names Israel and Sara have clearly later been added to the typewritten documents in handwriting. There are also fingerprints and an exemption from work until further notice – understandable, considering they were 76 and 66 years old respectively!

February 1941: *Joodsche Raad voor Amsterdam* (the *Judenrat* or Jewish Council) was established in Amsterdam by the Nazis to receive the German commands and to execute their orders. Two prominent Dutch Jews, Abraham Asscher, a diamond dealer, and Professor David Cohen headed the Jewish Council of 20 members. The Jewish Council also published a weekly newspaper, *Het Joodsche Weekblad*, which listed the many new laws and general prohibitions for Jews.

May 1941: Jews were not allowed to possess wireless sets and were forced to hand them in. Telephones in Jewish homes were cut off.

September 1941: Jewish behaviour in public: Jews were not allowed to visit parks, zoos, cafes, restaurants, hotels, theatres, concerts, libraries, museums, sports meetings, etc. This prompted the appearance of the official posters, *Voor Jooden verboden* – 'For Jews Prohibited' – at the entrances to shops, parks, swimming baths etc. This was also the start of sporadic roundups of young Jewish men, who were sent to Mauthausen Concentration Camp in Austria.

September 1941: Jewish children were not allowed into schools also attended by non-Jewish children.

January 1942: Jews were only allowed to reside in Amsterdam and they were not allowed outside the city boundary.

At the same time, in January 1942, the Nazis decided on *Die Endlösung der Judenfrage* (The Final Solution of the Jewish Question) at the Wannsee Conference, just outside Berlin. Effectively, this was the beginning of the systematic liquidation of all Jews living in Germany and the occupied territories. Of course, we were totally unaware of this plan and we never even knew about it until after the war. It was not long, however, before we experienced the first stages of the 'Final Solution'. The first step for us was to move to Amsterdam on 2 May 1942. Although we were allowed to take all our possessions, the flat in Amsterdam was much smaller and we had to leave some furniture behind, such as our piano, which was placed in the church for 'safe-keeping'.

PREPARED FOR DEPORTATION
Amsterdam. May 1942 – June 1943.

Amsterdam was founded in 1275 and since the 17th Century there has been a Jewish area in Amsterdam. The *Joodenbuurt* (Jewish area) greatly contributed to the city's language, humour, culture and character. Over many years Jewish immigrants had settled in this area, just southeast of the centre of the city, and most of the established Dutch Jewish families lived there. It was never a ghetto, but the surrounding canals and bridges enabled it to be easily isolated. Local Jews were particularly active in the street markets and in the thriving diamond industry. Dutch Jews owned many of the Dutch companies and stores. The Jews of Holland tended to be orthodox or secular. All of them were fully integrated citizens of Holland.

At the time of the German invasion in May 1940, there were about 140,000 Jews in Holland, including some 30,000 Jewish refugees from Germany. About half of all the Jews lived in

Amsterdam. In 1942, the Nazis concentrated the entire Jewish population in Amsterdam.

When we were ordered to move to Amsterdam in May 1942, we did not move to the *Joodenbuurt*. Instead, we went to live in the relatively new southern part of Amsterdam, the so-called *Rivierenbuurt* (Rivers area) because the streets were named after Dutch rivers. We lived at 163/II Vechtstraat, Amsterdam-Zuid, on the second storey of a typical Dutch apartment block. Many other Jewish families lived in this area, especially Jewish refugees from Germany, who introduced the German brand of liberal Judaism to Holland. We lived not far from the Frank family from Frankfurt. Anne was a year younger than me, and although I do not remember meeting her at the time, our paths would cross again later.

As we were close to the Amsterdam city boundary, we could walk to the river Amstel and see the surrounding countryside. Later, such visits were prohibited to Jews. Life was becoming distinctly uncomfortable and there was a regular procession of more and more anti-Jewish decrees, aimed to humiliate, separate and isolate the Jewish community from the Dutch population and to restrict their freedom of movement, which would directly affect all of us.

Here is a summary of the growing list of decrees in chronological order, following those we already experienced in Naarden:

April 1942: Jews had to wear the Jewish star, a yellow piece of cloth imprinted in black with the Star of David and the Dutch word *'JOOD'*, which means 'JEW', on the left side of the breast on the outer clothing. The star had to be purchased for four cents and a 1/4 clothing coupon, as you were not allowed to make your own star. The clearly visible yellow star made it easier for the Germans to enforce their anti-Jewish restrictions and was supposed to be another humiliation for the Jews. However, many Dutch citizens actually regarded the star as a badge of honour, and they would smile, and bow and raise their hats.

May 1942: Money, bank balances, stocks and shares, life insurance policies and other securities had to be deposited with Lippmann, Rosenthal & Co, a special 'Jewish' bank, which the Nazis eventually confiscated.

June 1942: Jewish houses, property, companies and businesses were placed under German supervision or liquidated.

June 1942: Jews were not allowed out between 8pm and 6am the following morning.

July 1942: Furniture, antiques, jewellery and vehicles were confiscated, including bicycles, our last means of transport. As soon as a Jewish family had been deported, a special removals company called A. Puls would empty their home and transport all contents to Germany.

July 1942: Jews were only permitted to enter non-Jewish shops between the designated hours of 3pm and 5pm and were not allowed to go to the hairdresser. Jews were prohibited from visiting non-Jewish homes and only allowed to travel with a special permit.

July 1942: This was the start of the forced deportation of Jews from Holland. Jews between the ages of 16 and 45 were 'invited' to come forward for resettlement in the east or for forced labour in Germany. This was later supplemented by lists of Jews to be deported, prepared by the Jewish Council and eventually by random arrests in the streets and by *razzias* (mass roundups) in local areas of Amsterdam.

FROM BELSEN TO BUCKINGHAM PALACE

August 1942: Jews who did not come forward for forced labour in Germany, or who did not wear the obligatory Jewish star, or who changed residence without permission (i.e. went into hiding), would be deported to the Mauthausen Concentration Camp in Austria. Mauthausen soon gained a very bad reputation. Relatives would receive an official note that so-and-so had died in Mauthausen of a 'heart attack' and their ashes could be purchased.

October 1942: Eventually, the Jews in Holland were effectively outlawed and only those with valid exemptions were allowed to remain in Amsterdam. Block by block, the Jews were being rounded up and deported from the city. Most of the Jews from Holland were sent to the Westerbork Transit Camp and from there to Auschwitz, Sobibor, Bergen-Belsen and Theresienstadt. Out of the 140,000 Jews living in Holland at the time of the German invasion in 1940, only 35,000 survived.

This time, for several reasons, I was better able to appreciate the effect of all these anti-Jewish decrees, and the reaction from the Jewish and non-Jewish population, than when I was in Berlin. Firstly, I was probably too young in Berlin and I only experienced the earlier decrees until the beginning of 1936. Now I was 12 years old and was actually personally affected. Secondly, during our time in Berlin, there was always the prospect of emigration. There was no such option in Holland.

My impression of the Jewish reaction is that the step-by-step introduction of these anti-Jewish laws caused people to accept each new decree with a certain amount of equanimity. They had managed to survive all the previous decrees, and hence were prepared to cope with every new decree, hoping it would be the final one. Furthermore, the Nazis were very clever in persuading the Jewish Council to administer these decrees. The Dutch Jews were also great optimists: "One or two months before the war is over and then we are free!" Mr Asscher of the Jewish Council said when the yellow star was introduced.

The non-Jewish Dutch population was a great source of support. Most of them hated the Germans almost as much as we did. They called them *Rot-Moffen*, ('rotten Krauts' or 'rotten Jerries') because the Germans had occupied their country and caused shortages of food, heating and clothing. We had many Dutch friends, who were always prepared to help us in any way they could. This aspect was very different in, say, Germany, Hungary or Poland, where the majority of the local population favoured the Nazis rather than the Jews. In fact, the lack of protest in Germany, instilled by fear and intimidation, may have encouraged the Nazis to implement the same anti-Jewish laws in other countries.

It has been said that many good people ignored what was happening to the Jews, first in Germany, and later in Holland and in other occupied countries. However in Holland, the non-Jewish population did attempt to protest and did take action. For example, right at the beginning of the anti-Jewish measures, in February 1941, there was a general strike in Holland, led by the dock workers. Order was brutally restored within two days by SS reprisals, involving the execution or deportation of numerous innocent young men who had earlier been picked up at random in the streets.

There was also a Dutch underground resistance movement, with illegal printing presses and prohibited newspapers. But it was not enough, and by then it was probably impossible to stop or reverse the liquidation programme of the Jews. Many among the Dutch population opposed the Nazi regime and several Dutch families and individuals helped and supported those local Jews who had gone into hiding. A disproportionate number of Dutch names have been recognised in the 'Avenue of the Righteous Among the Nations' at the Yad Vashem Memorial in Jerusalem.

We lived in Amsterdam for nearly 14 months. This was quite a long time considering the circumstances. The transports to Westerbork started in July 1942, but we avoided deportation for month after month, during which time many tens of thousands of Jews were sent to the camps. In Amsterdam, as in Naarden, we were not permitted to attend non-Jewish schools, and I attended the *Joodse HBS* (Jewish secondary grammar school) near the Weesperplein by the old Jewish quarter. I only remember this because I have my class report for the summer term of 1942, showing eight out of ten for Hebrew and Religious Studies. This is obviously where, as a 14-year-old, I really started to learn about Judaism for the first time. For some reason, I was very much into Greek mythology: the Trojan horse, the Odyssey and other wonderful stories about the Greek gods. I spent much time reading in those days. It was one of the few pastimes that were not restricted. Apart from educational books, I remember some unusual detective stories based on cartoons – an early version of the post-war comics. The only other subject that I remember from our days in Amsterdam is sports. We were not allowed to play football but we were allowed to play mixed hockey, and I did, although we were not allowed to play with or against non-Jews. I also played table tennis for the first time in Amsterdam. After the war, I spent many years playing league table tennis in Birmingham.

It is strange that I can remember very few people from Amsterdam, whereas I can remember many names and faces from

PREPARED FOR DEPORTATION

Heemstede and from Naarden. On reflection, it was probably due to the limited contact we had with other people. We were not permitted to associate with non-Jews and most Jews tried to keep a low profile. We were not allowed into most places, and so therefore stayed at home. Incidentally, each of us had several yellow stars, stitched to our coats, jackets and pullovers. The yellow star had to be visible at all times.

One dreadful feature that I do remember was the arrival each morning at school to see who was missing of children and teachers. Classes were diminishing rapidly as a result of these nightly roundups and deportations. Most people were picked up during the night, when the curfew was in force, and all Jews had to be at their home address. The nights became very frightening as we spent many sleepless hours, listening for strange noises, waiting to be picked up, hoping that nothing would happen. Perhaps these were some of the worst times, when we were just waiting, every night, for something terrible to happen – knowing that eventually it would. This was the kind of nightmare that, later in my life, I never wanted my children to experience.

We managed to stay in Amsterdam throughout 1942 and into 1943 because my father, after losing his job at the Mendelssohn Bank when it was seized by the Nazis, was working for the Jewish Council as an inspector in the Information Service, which helped Jews to complete the necessary forms with their financial information. Full-time members of the Jewish Council and their co-operators were exempt from the deportations and at one time about 25,000 co-operators, including my father, were attached to the Jewish Council. Everybody used whatever influence they had, or whatever opportunity that arose, to gain exemption from the dreaded deportations.

FROM BELSEN TO BUCKINGHAM PALACE

My father had registered Eve as a British subject with the Swiss Embassy in Amsterdam in June 1942 as, obviously, there was no British Embassy in Holland during the German occupation. After consultation with the British Foreign Office in London via the British Embassy in Switzerland, the Swiss Embassy in Amsterdam confirmed in September 1942 that Eve was indeed a British citizen, and therefore not subject to certain Nazi laws such as wearing the yellow star. Almost a year later, in March 1943, the Swiss Embassy informed my father that Eve and her immediate family might possibly be exchanged for German citizens interned in Great Britain. This was a major achievement for my father, which would eventually save the lives of some of us. I have a list of the correspondence between my father and the Swiss Embassy and the Red Cross, but not the actual letters. Although Eve was born in London, and we had a copy of her birth certificate, she never had a British passport; we have heard of similar cases, where the Germans would not recognise a British subject without a British passport. Furthermore, since both Eve's parents were German at the time of her birth, she could also be classified as 'German', or of dual nationality. Because Eve had a British birth certificate, we always stayed together as a family. I don't believe that our parents ever considered splitting up, whereby each of us might separately go into hiding with appropriate friends in Holland.

My father did well to get the British and the Germans to acknowledge Eve as a British citizen. He was not aware that our fate had been sealed at the German Foreign Office, which had devised an *'exchange plan'* early in 1943 in order to repatriate German citizens from all over the world, whereby Jews with dual nationality who also possessed British or American citizenship might be exchanged for Germans interned within the British or American spheres of influence; therefore, these Jews should be exempted from the normal measures taken against other Jews. In principle, this plan was agreed at the very highest levels by von Ribbentrop, Himmler and Hitler himself, although various amendments were later proposed and accepted.

The brutal winter of 1942/43 was also difficult for the Dutch population under the German occupation because the Germans were shipping vast quantities of food to Germany itself. Coal for heating was scarce, both food and clothing was rationed, there were acute shortages and a thriving black market developed. But everything was far more difficult for the remaining Jews in Amsterdam. For example, by the time Jews were allowed into shops in the afternoon, most items were sold out. We tried to use Eve, who was six years old at the time, to do our shopping for us. She did not have to wear the yellow star because she was British. We told her what to get and gave her the money to pay for it, but she had difficulty in remembering what to ask for without reference to us, standing outside the shop with our yellow stars and liable to be arrested for such devious tactics. The Dutch population was able to travel out of Amsterdam and obtain food directly from farms and countryside shops. This was far more difficult and dangerous for Jews, who were not allowed to travel outside Amsterdam and who did not possess extra money or exchange products. Nevertheless, my mother and Ruzzi did manage to supplement our food rations. Using rowing boats to cross the Amstel river, they sold our surplus clothing and jewellery to enable them to barter for bread and milk.

By this time, the remaining Jewish families in Amsterdam could see the regular deportations to Westerbork and realised that it was only a matter of time before we would all be caught. Block by block, the Jews were being rounded up and deported from the city by train. There was no sign of an early end to the war and our exemptions and a certain amount of luck would only protect us for a limited time. There was one other option which might save us from deportation, and which was used by many Jewish families: we could go into hiding (in Dutch *'onder-duiken'*: literally, 'diving under the water'), either in Amsterdam or somewhere in the countryside. Unfortunately, Holland was not an ideal country for hiding. It was small, it was flat, and it had a long border with Germany, the arch-enemy.

To hide from the Germans, and their sympathisers in Holland, you needed Dutch non-Jewish friends who could offer a hiding place and who were prepared to take the risks associated with such ventures. The Germans were well aware of this procedure and they made it quite clear that any Dutch citizens caught helping or hiding Jews would be shot or sent to a concentration camp. On the other hand, there was a reward for reporting Jews in hiding.

Obviously people did not advertise their intention to go into hiding. Suddenly, quietly, they would disappear. They would no longer attend school, they would no longer be in the streets or shops. Often, we would not know whether they had gone into hiding or had been arrested and deported.

Nevertheless, there were many brave Dutch people who were prepared to hide their Jewish friends. The vast majority of the Dutch population hated the Germans, who had occupied their country, conscripted their young men, caused food and clothing shortages and generally subjected Holland to a regime of terror. In our case, my parents had many Dutch Christian friends who offered to help us, in particular a lady who lived in the flat below us; 'Tante Fie', Mrs S. Koster, who was especially friendly with Eve. I believe that my mother might have been prepared to go into hiding and take the associated risks, but my father argued against any such plans. He had been brought up as a good German, who always obeyed the rules. He was a disciplinarian with a strong personality. His education and training had conditioned him to do as he was told and then everything would be all right. He had always lived by these principles, but he now faced a life-and-death dilemma, a situation for which he was totally unprepared. At 40 years of age, he probably found it difficult to change the habits of a lifetime, and so he rejected the idea of breaking the law and going into hiding.

Apparently some 24,000 Jews in Holland went into hiding, both in the cities and in the countryside, where there was more food and fewer police. In retrospect it is difficult to say, even today, whether we would have been better off following this course of action. We might have all survived. Sixteen thousand Jews in hiding in Holland did survive, but if we had been caught like Anne Frank and her family, we might all have perished in Auschwitz.

It has been reported that the Allies knew about Hitler's 'Final Solution', and about Auschwitz and the gas chambers in 1942. If so, it is most unfortunate that there appeared to have been no warnings to the Jews in occupied Europe; we may have been able to move to avoid the deportations to the death camps and subsequent catastrophes. So, as thousands of Jews were transported to Westerbork every month, we remained in Amsterdam; Father at the Jewish Council, Mother and Eve at home, Ruzzi and me at school. Ruzzi went to a Jewish school in the Jekerstraat, possibly the same school that Anne Frank attended, although Ruzzi was two years younger than Anne and did not knowingly meet her.

FROM BELSEN TO BUCKINGHAM PALACE

Our four grandparents, meanwhile, had also been forced to leave Heemstede and they were living in the *Joodse Invalide*, the principal Jewish old-people's home in Amsterdam. We were able to visit them regularly, but in March 1943 the entire building was evacuated and all the aged inhabitants, many of them sick, maimed or dying, were sent to Westerbork.

The deportation of the remaining Jews from Amsterdam accelerated in the spring of 1943. There were *razzias* during the daytime, when Jews would be arrested in the streets. In the evenings or at night, Jews were taken from their homes. The biggest house-to-house raids were on 26 May in the central areas of Amsterdam and on 20 June in the southern and eastern parts of the city. Approximately 10,000 Jews were caught in each of these raids. The latter raid included our family. This was our real day of horror, our black Sunday, which totally changed our way of life forever.

It was very early on Sunday morning, 20 June 1943, before people were up and about, and whilst the curfew was still in force. The whole area of southeast Amsterdam was cordoned off by the SS, assisted by the German Army and the Dutch police in military vehicles. No one was allowed to pass in or out. Being a Sunday morning, there was no reason for Dutch people to go to work as they did not work on Sundays in those days. There was no way out for us, not even across the Amstel river.

Loudspeakers were issuing commands to the Jewish residents and officers from the *Grüne Polizei* ('Green Police') – German military police – were knocking on the doors of all Jewish homes. They hammered on our door, checked our names and told us to assemble at the top of our street within 30 minutes, for transportation to a camp. They stood and waited in our apartment until we were ready to depart. My parents were obviously shocked and my father referred to his exemption from the Jewish Council, but the officers ignored it. It turned out later that the Jewish Council stamps were of no further value. In fact, the entire Jewish Council was arrested and deported two months later. My father also referred to Eve's British nationality, but the officers refused any discussion and told us to get ready for departure. It was the end of our life 'at home' in a house or flat. For the next two years we would be living in camps, in barracks, with hundreds and thousands of fellow sufferers. It was the end of our private life with our parents as a family.

We did not panic, and there was no shouting or crying. We knew that this would happen one day, although we prayed that it should not happen. We had been prepared for this event for many months, and there had been detailed instructions on what food and clothing to take along to the camps for each person, in case we were separated: one suitcase or rucksack, one pair of work boots, two pairs of socks, two underpants, two shirts, one pullover, two woollen blankets, two sets of bed linen, one eating bowl, one drinking mug, one spoon and cutlery, plus towels, toilet articles, food for three days and no pets. We wore our best and our warmest clothing in double layers, so that we did not have to carry them, and we could bring other items in our suitcases. We were very hot, because it was a fine summer's day in June.

Our suitcases and rucksacks, clearly marked with first name, family name, date of birth and 'Holland' as prescribed, had been ready for months. Now my mother collected the remaining food and emergency rations from the kitchen and my father assembled relevant papers; each of us had a small cloth pouch (like a modern money-belt) which my mother had made, which we carried around our necks. Each of these contained a copy of Eve's birth certificate, other documents and valuables, and some money. Most of our valuables, prized possessions and documents, including photographs and certificates, had long ago been entrusted to various Dutch non-Jewish friends for safe-keeping until after the war. This is how we came to possess most of the articles mentioned in this book. For example, my father's piano was 'lent' to the church in Naarden. We saw it after the war, but never claimed it back. Our Märklin electric train, Leica camera, best silver cutlery etc. were all hidden with Dutch friends and were recovered after the war.

Even at this very last moment, Tante Fie, living below us, offered to hide us in her apartment. But it was too late and might have been fatal for her. We heard, after the war, that the police officers had actually missed our front door, but a Dutch Nazi sympathiser from across the road advised them of their mistake and they came back for us.

We went down the stairs of our apartment block for the last time, waved goodbye to our friends, and carried our luggage to the assembly area at the top of our street. My father used his German language to plead once more with the Gestapo and senior SS officers, referring to his Jewish Council stamp and to Eve's British nationality, but to no avail. There were many other Jewish families and school friends, but not much conversation. When everyone had been assembled we filed into the waiting tram cars, which were usually out of bounds for Jews, and were taken to the nearby Muiderpoort railway station. There, literally thousands of other Jews were being collected that morning. Slowly, everyone filed towards the station platforms, where we had our first sight of the infamous cattle wagons. We climbed into the wagons with our luggage, together with many other families. When the wagon was full, the doors were closed and locked from the outside.

It was about midday. The operation in Amsterdam had taken all morning. There was lots of standing around and waiting, and everything had happened in a very slow and orderly fashion. It was all very depressing and there was a general mood of resignation. There was no shouting or beating or shooting, and there was no attempt at resistance against the overwhelming odds. We knew that we would be deported to a camp, and that it would obviously be worse than living in Amsterdam, but we had no idea what to expect.

There was always a general fear of the unknown, but we resigned ourselves to our fate. (Life in Amsterdam had deteriorated during 1942 and 1943, and it would get worse in 1944; 20,000 Dutch citizens would die of starvation in Holland during the winter of 1944/45.) But our parents still believed that Eve's British nationality would eventually prove beneficial.

At last our train started to move and we travelled for several hours. There was daylight inside the wagon, but we could not see outside. It was a journey that was full of speculation and fear. When the train finally stopped and the doors were opened, we had arrived in Westerbork. It was 20 June 1943, and we started what was to become a new and terrifying episode in our lives.

IN TRANSIT

Westerbork. June 1943 – February 1944.

Lager (camp) Westerbork was situated in a desolate heathland area in northeast Holland, just south of the town of Assert and not far from the German border. It was built in 1939 by the Dutch authorities to provide shelter for homeless Jewish refugees from Germany. After the German occupation of Holland in 1940, the camp was taken over by the Germans as a transit camp from which they could deport Jews to the east. The camp was nearly half a mile square, surrounded by a moat, a barbed wire fence and watchtowers. But Westerbork was never a concentration camp and certainly not an extermination camp. Nobody died in Westerbork, except from natural causes. There was no starvation and there was no disease. The food was adequate and, until the end of 1943, could be supplemented by food parcels from outside the camp. There were well-equipped medical facilities and many excellent Jewish doctors and nurses. Brick-built houses and bungalows with front gardens and flowers, built for and occupied by the original veteran German refugees, were supplemented by huge wooden barracks to house the many thousands of Jews in transit to the east. At times, more than 15,000 people stayed in Westerbork, leading to severe overcrowding in the barracks. Eventually, more than 100,000 people were deported from there to the concentration and extermination camps in Germany and Poland.

When our train arrived in Westerbork on the afternoon of 20 June 1943, the doors of the cattle wagons were opened and we disembarked inside the camp. We then waited in a long queue to be registered by the Jewish camp inmate administrators, sitting behind a long line of tables using typewriters to record our personal details and prepare our *Ausweiskarten* (registration cards). Eventually we were assigned to our barracks. There were separate barracks for men and women; my mother, Eve, who was now seven years old, and Ruzzi, aged 11, went to Barracks 57 while my father and I, now 14 years old, were housed in Barracks 85 and subsequently Barracks 83. Later, we would be moved nearer each other in Barracks 65 and 68 respectively. We separated our luggage appropriately and examined our new homes. Each barracks comprised several rows of tall iron bedsteads with three levels of bunk beds, each with straw sacks. As many as 800 people could be housed in each one. Suitcases were stored underneath the bunk beds. The top bunks offered most space, but required a certain agility to reach. People were hanging their clothes and laundry from convenient hooks and lines inside the barracks. There were no proper living rooms, dining areas, or toilet facilities, but there were some wooden tables and benches, a communal wash area and some cast iron heating stoves inside, and external toilet huts. The toilet huts comprised double rows of ten seats without partitions.

IN TRANSIT

We soon learned to abandon all ideas of privacy. Food was distributed three times a day. There were also administration buildings, kitchens, a laundry and even a bath-house inside the camp. There was a general curfew at 8pm, lights went out at 10pm, and we had to get up at 6am. I somehow still have my last *Badekarte* from Westerbork, when my allocated bath time was 3pm every Friday afternoon. The back of the card has been stamped on 1, 7, 14, 21 and 28 January 1944. After the war, my family was suitably impressed that I had actually taken a bath every week. I did not realise it at the time, but these were my last bath sessions for more than a year.

The German camp commandant, SS *Obersturmführer* Konrad Gemmeker, his staff, and the Dutch military police guarding the camp all lived just outside the fence. The camp was administered by another Jewish Council, made up primarily of the original German Jewish refugee camp inhabitants under the notorious leadership of Kurt Schlesinger. Like the Jewish Council in Amsterdam, this group of Jewish 'elders' would be responsible for discipline and cleanliness and enforcing the German commands, in return for certain privileges in terms of food, housing and, most importantly, exemption from the regular transports. They prepared the dreaded weekly lists of people selected for 'resettlement in the east', the euphemism used by the Germans to denote the deportations to the death camps. In Westerbork, we still believed the German propaganda, thinking that we would be sent to labour camps in Eastern Europe to work for the Germans; that families would not be separated; and if we behaved ourselves and did as we were told, everything would be all right. In retrospect, we must have been a bit naïve. Why would the Germans send old-age pensioners and young children, grandparents and grandchildren, pregnant women and mothers with babies, invalids and sick people to work for the Germans in labour camps in the east? Perhaps we wanted to believe this German version of our fate, as we certainly had no idea what was really happening at the destinations of the transports from Westerbork.

It may be interesting to speculate what might have happened if we had known the true destination of the transports and the fate of those on board. I believe that we might well have taken some kind of action, rather than meekly and willingly wait for our turn to be deported. This may not have been possible in Auschwitz or even in Bergen-Belsen, but in Westerbork, resistance or escape could have been arranged. The supervision was not too strict and most of the prisoners were relatively fit and in good health, and some form of concerted action might well have succeeded. For this reason, the Germans tended to rule the camp with kid gloves, in order not to provoke friction and resistance among the prisoners. They also took great care not to disclose the real purpose of the transports. In consequence, we were not sufficiently desperate to escape – knowing that escape from Westerbork into the Dutch countryside was effectively the same as going into hiding. It meant removing our yellow stars and asking Dutch people to risk their lives by providing food and shelter for us. Many of us had rejected this option before, so why risk it now with complete strangers who might denounce us to the authorities? Furthermore, escape was only practicable for individuals, not for families with children. As soon as an escape was confirmed, his or her family in Westerbork would be deported on the next transport to the east, together with ten other inmates from the same barracks.

Every Monday evening a train with about 20 cattle wagons

would enter the camp and, later that evening, a list of approximately 1,000 people would be published by the Jewish Council. In each barracks, the appropriate names would be called out by the barracks leader and these unfortunate people had to assemble by the railway siding inside the camp next morning. Obviously, Monday evenings were just terrible. Everyone was in their barracks, waiting for the names to be called. The anxiety mounted, then everyone fell silent. The lists were in alphabetical order, so there was a build-up of tension as your letter approached – and an overwhelming sense of relief when your letter had passed by, without your name being called. But others would be crying, weeping and consoling. The named deportees started packing their remaining belongings, perhaps to divert their anxieties.

The fine and respectable people on the weekly list would assemble by the train early on Tuesday morning. After verification of their names and numbers, they would enter the wagons, at least 50 persons per wagon together with one bucket of water and another for toilet purposes, ignorant of their fate. The doors would be closed and locked from the outside, and the train departed punctually at 11am with its human cargo, for the long journey to its unknown destination in the east. The vast majority would be dead within 24 hours of arrival at its destination.

The week in Westerbork went from Monday evening to Monday evening. If you survived Monday, then you would be safe for another seven days. As in Amsterdam, where everyone applied to the Jewish Council for exemption from deportation, the same was happening in Westerbork. Everyone tried to use their influence with the Westerbork Jewish Council, and tried desperately to be allowed to stay. Everyone was convinced that deportation to another camp was going to be worse in the same way that every previous forced move had led to worse conditions. This assumption was absolutely correct, but no one realised just how much worse it would be.

When we arrived in Westerbork in June 1943, we immediately looked for our grandparents who had been evacuated from the *Joodse Invalide* in Amsterdam in March 1943, and we were delighted to find the Oppenheimer grandparents (my father's parents) still living there. It was almost a joyful reunion, considering the circumstances. Alas, the Fürst grandparents (my mother's parents) had been deported almost immediately after their arrival, and we never heard from them again. The Oppenheimer grandparents were on the weekly list only four weeks after our arrival. My father went to see the Jewish Council in Westerbork and pleaded for his parents, but there was nothing he could do to remove their names from the list and next morning they disappeared on the train to the east.

After the war, I examined the official German records in the archives of the Yad Vashem Holocaust Museum in Jerusalem and found that all four grandparents were murdered on arrival in Sobibor, the Fürsts on 26 March 1943 and the Oppenheimers on 23 July 1943 (see Appendix 2). The sheer thoroughness with which the Nazis meticulously documented their crimes, as blandly and as fastidiously as any administrative government department, is almost unbelievable. The records show that 34,313 named persons were deported from Westerbork to Sobibor and only 19 survived the gas chambers in this notorious killing centre. This is the equivalent of deporting one entire large secondary school of about 1,000 pupils every week – and every other week one single child would survive ... all the others were murdered.... This was even worse than Auschwitz: 58,380 Jews from Westerbork went there and 854 survived. All in all, 93 trains left Westerbork at weekly intervals, between July 1942 and September 1944. The Frank family was on the last transport to Auschwitz. More than 100,000 prisoners were deported from Westerbork, less than 5,000 (1 in 20) survived, mostly from Theresienstadt and Bergen-Belsen.

Meanwhile, we remained in Westerbork week after week, and we were never on the dreaded Monday evening lists. This was not just a matter of luck. We had been allowed to remain in Amsterdam because my father worked for the Jewish Council. Now we were allowed to remain in Westerbork because my sister Eve was born in England. We noticed that our Westerbork registration cards carried a blue 'exemption' stamp. Many other families in Westerbork also had such stamps and none of their names appeared on the weekly deportation lists. It soon became apparent that many blue stamp families included British or American subjects, and we concluded that the Nazis wanted to exchange us for German nationals interned in Britain and America, as intimated by the Swiss Embassy in their letter of March 1943. This assumption proved to be correct and there were rumours that the Nazis wanted five or even ten Germans (preferably military POWs) for each one of us Jews. No wonder we were never exchanged!

There might have been another reason why British and American nationals were not deported to the east. If the Allies had found out that any of their citizens had been sent to Auschwitz and deliberately murdered, then they might have taken reprisals against German citizens living in Britain and America. Some individuals with British or American passports were sent from Westerbork to a Red Cross internment camp in Vittel in France, better known today for its mineral water. Conditions were

Identity cards carried by my father's parents.
They clearly indicate the large letter J and bear the names 'Israel' and 'Sara'.
They were both deported to Sobibor, 1943.

My mother's last letter, sent from Westerbork in 1943.
See appendix 4 for full text.

My bath card. Every Friday at 3pm I had to report to the bath house. The card shows I had a bath on 1, 7, 14, 21, and 28 January 1944.

My work card from Westerbork. It actually documents when I was not there on the reverse, with a substantial number of sick days being listed.

The Allied Expeditionary Forces issued Displaced Persons cards to survivors of the camps. This was the only confirmation of our status at the time.

considered better than in Westerbork and some of them were eventually exchanged. There were many other families with other coloured stamps in Westerbork; most of them had British entry visas for Palestine or for various South and Central American countries. My father had also tried to obtain visas for Palestine for all of us (and for his parents) from his younger sister, Liesl, who had emigrated to Palestine during the 1930s. Correspondence between ourselves, the Red Cross and the Swiss Embassy in Holland confirms the dates of our applications, but I do not believe we were ever issued the actual visas. Many other Jewish families did obtain their visas and subsequent blue stamps in Westerbork.

There were other families, with other coloured stamps on their identity cards, who were able to postpone their deportation 'until further notice', such as the Jewish members of the Dutch diamond industry and those Jews involved in the entertainment in Westerbork, as well as doctors and nurses who worked in the hospital. Obviously not everyone was equal, and many had some kind of exemption from the regular deportations. We knew very few people there, though. My best friends were all non-Jewish in Heemstede and in Naarden, but I cannot remember a single Jewish friend from Amsterdam. In Westerbork, and later in Bergen-Belsen, we had to start all over again to make new friends.

I spent my 15th birthday in the camp. We missed the comforts of home life that our parents had been able to provide, but there were facilities for sports such as athletics, boxing, football and a weekly entertainment including cinema, concerts and theatre. Married couples could even hire a room for lovemaking. There was an excellent cabaret company and an orchestra, and all the best actors, musicians and boxers were exempt from the weekly transports to the east. It was a tremendous incentive to perform, and to perform well in front of the SS officers in the audience.

Westerbork had its own printed currency, which looked similar to Monopoly money. There was a shop and a post office which sold the special pre-printed 'Lager Westerbork' stationery. We were not allowed to leave the camp or entertain visitors from outside, but we could write to Dutch friends in Holland and we could ask them to send us food and/or clothing. At a later stage, the letters and the parcels were rationed. Finally, towards the end of 1943, parcels could only be sent by relatives or Jewish friends, in accordance with a complicated *zegel* (label) system which effectively terminated the receipt of parcels and correspondence.

I have some of the Westerbork letters my father and mother wrote to their colleagues and friends, which I recovered after the war. It is quite emotional to read what turned out to be their last letters. My father wrote in German, my mother in Dutch, asking for pyjamas, *siroop* (cough mixture), a Bible and my Jewish study book. In a postcard from my father, he asks for a Bible and some shaving soap, and weekly supplementary food parcels (up to 2 kg). "We are alright here," he says; "we hope it will not get worse ... we are in good health." These were their last written words, knowing that all correspondence would be censored (Appendix 4).

All inmates over the age of 14 had to work in Westerbork. Although I was only 14 years old on arrival, I was classified as an adult, and therefore liable to work. My duties were never very arduous, mainly agricultural, like harvesting potatoes. But I was exposed to the elements and subject to many colds, coughs and sneezes, as witnessed by my *Arbeitskarte* (work card) which shows that I was signed off as medically unfit to work on 19 occasions for a total of 42 days during my seven months there. On every occasion, I received two or three days of BR (bed rest) or DF (duty free). My parents both had to work in Westerbork, but I cannot recall what duties they performed. We all met up at lunchtime and in the evening to have our meals together. Ruzzi and Eve (13 and 7 years old, respectively) may have had some ad hoc school lessons and Jewish education during the day, but the regular deportation of both students and teachers made it impossible to maintain a structured timetable of lessons despite many valiant attempts. In Westerbork, Ruzzi started to learn the importance of scavenging. He collected scraps of food outside the kitchens and noted the food distribution procedures. In many ways, it was an excellent training ground for our life in less favourable camps.

All in all, life in Westerbork was not intolerable, providing you were exempt from the weekly transports. By now, according to our underground information service, the Germans had been defeated at El Alamein and at Stalingrad, and the Allies had landed in Italy. Apparently, Hitler was losing the war and we were beginning to hope that we might survive in Westerbork.

Unfortunately, this situation changed abruptly in January 1944. First, a high-ranking Nazi Party official, one Fräulein Slottke – from the political department of Jewish Affairs within the Security Police (Gestapo) office in The Hague – arrived to check the credentials of all the people with exemption stamps. Apparently, many of the documents were false. They were divided into two categories: prominent Jews who had served in high office in Holland or Germany would be sent to Theresienstadt; Jews destined for 'exchange' purposes would be sent for internment to Bergen-Belsen. This confirmed our earlier suspicions and attendant rumours. There was indeed a high-level diplomatic exchange plan. Early in January 1944, in Westerbork, we received an official letter announcing a decision on our application for internment. We would be sent to Bergen-Belsen – our fate had been determined in Berlin. This was the first time that we heard the name Bergen-Belsen, but we were aware that we were privileged to be sent there rather than to Auschwitz, which was already gaining a bad reputation.

When the weekly train arrived in the camp on the following Monday evening, 10 January 1944, the train consisted of third-class passenger coaches with doors and windows and seats, not the usual cattle wagons – and before we had a chance to determine the reason for this novelty, the Monday evening list was published. It comprised more than 1,000 persons as usual, but all had coloured stamps on their registration cards and were destined for Bergen-Belsen

We were not on the list that evening, but the passenger coaches augured well for our future. Naturally, there was much speculation among the remaining coloured stamp holders in Westerbork, also destined for Bergen-Belsen, hoping for an actual exchange to freedom.

Yet there was always the fear of the unknown. Despite the promises and propaganda, most people preferred to stay where they were. And sure enough, the same routine happened three weeks later on 31 January 1944, and this time all five Oppenheimers were on the transport list.

Our names were duly called out in Barracks 65 and 68 that evening. We packed our limited amount of food and clothing into our suitcases and rucksacks and spent a last, uneasy night in Westerbork, wondering where we were going and what was going to happen to us. Next morning we assembled by the train at the railway siding inside the camp. More than 900 coloured stamp holders, in family groups, were called up this time. There was a mood of apprehension as we climbed into the train, all five of us together, with our luggage. The train doors were not even locked – we were quick to spot good and bad omens. But when the train departed, it stopped outside the camp and the doors were locked.

It was the afternoon of Tuesday 1 February 1944 when the train left Westerbork. It was almost dark by the time we crossed the border into Germany. After a slow and tedious journey in an easterly direction, taking many hours to travel less than 200 miles through the bleak terrain of northwest Germany in mid-winter, we arrived early next morning at a railway siding in open countryside. The trains did not go into Bergen-Belsen as in Westerbork. There was no station and no place name. There was only a ramp (raised platform) for disembarkation – and there was a 'welcoming party' of SS officers, guards and other military personnel with machine guns and vicious dogs. It did not look good and it looked even worse when we had carried our luggage two or three miles down the road to the actual camp. So this was Bergen-Belsen. We had never heard of it before Fräulein Slottke mentioned it, and told us we were privileged to go there, but we could see straightaway that it was much worse than Westerbork, and nothing like the attractive 'exchange camp' we had envisaged in our dreams.

FINAL DESTINATION
Bergen-Belsen, February 1944 – April 1945

The Bergen-Belsen camp was located north of Hanover and near the town of Celle within the Lüneburg Heath in northwest Germany. Its name was derived from the nearby small town of Bergen and the village of Belsen, which comprised only a few farms and houses. There was a very large German Army camp nearby at Hohne, home of a Panzer tank division, which was taken over by the British Army after the war, and is still in use today.

The camp was surrounded by several rows of barbed wire, watchtowers manned by SS guards with machine guns, and searchlights. Anyone approaching the prohibited zones near the barbed wire was liable to be shot. There were also armed guards on patrol with vicious-looking Alsatian dogs and bloodhounds. The camp appeared to be larger than Westerbork, though we never had an opportunity to see the entire layout, with its maze of compounds and sub-compounds divided by high fences. The armed SS guards and officers belonged to the *Totenkopf* (Death's Head) division. They wore a skull insignia on their caps, jackets and drab olive-green uniforms. This was rather surprising to us, as the SS officers from our previous encounters in Berlin and Amsterdam all dressed in black uniforms and long leather jackboots, looking particularly sinister and intimidating.

Perhaps it is important to explain that Bergen-Belsen is somewhat of a paradox. Many people have portrayed Belsen as 'hell on earth' and the 'inferno of death' and the worst example of Nazi atrocities. This may be true of Belsen in 1945, and for those prisoners who came from other concentration camps, such as Auschwitz. But there was another, more lenient side to Bergen-Belsen, as described in this narrative, for the so-called 'exchange' Jews, and other privileged prisoners who lived in the Bergen-Belsen *Aufenthaltslager* (detention camp) in 1943/1944.

The camp was divided by a main road, more like a dirt track, running from east to west. The SS commandant and the guards lived at the eastern end of the road, outside the actual camp. Inside the camp, the kitchens and store rooms were on the northern side, faced by a series of compounds on the opposite southern side. The main camps, workshops, shoe tent and crematorium were at the western end of the main road.

Some of the first inmates of Bergen-Belsen in 1941 were Russian POWs, many of whom died in an early typhus epidemic.

In 1943, Bergen-Belsen became an *Aufenthaltslager* (detention camp) under the direct control of Himmler and the SS. In accordance with the plan to house 'exchange' Jews in Bergen-Belsen, it had been intended to call it a Civilian Internment Camp, but according to the Geneva Convention, this would have permitted visits from international committees such as the Red

Cross – which the Nazis did not want. Nevertheless, it was not a concentration camp at that time. The conditions in the camp were very much better than in a typical Nazi concentration camp, so that any subsequently exchanged prisoners would not be able to report on the real conditions inside such a place.

When we arrived in Bergen-Belsen on the morning of 2 February 1944, we were herded into one of the separate compounds of the detention camp called the *Austauschlager* (exchange camp). It was also referred to as the *Sternlager* (Star Camp), because the inhabitants were permitted to wear their civilian clothes with the yellow Jewish Star of David on the outside and were allowed to keep their luggage. All 'exchange' Jews lived in Bergen-Belsen as families, as in Westerbork, although men and women slept in different barracks. We did not have to wear the striped uniforms that the later arrivals from Auschwitz and other concentration camps were forced to wear. We observed several other separate compounds, which were all part of the detention camp, housing different categories of *Vorzugsjuden* ('preferential' or 'privileged' Jews). They were subject to different conditions. For example, there was the 'neutrals' camp for Jewish citizens from Spain and other neutral countries; a small camp for Jews from the Dutch diamond industry; another camp for a contingent of Jews from Hungary with kosher food and no work, also destined for exchange; and a 'special' camp for Polish Jews with South American papers or Palestine entry visas. These were all part of the exchange camp. They were not part of the POW camp nor part of the large area reserved for evacuees from the concentration camps, who arrived later in 1944 and in 1945. Quite recently, Bergen-Belsen has correctly been described as a 'multi-purpose camp'. However, the Germans did not permit any direct contact between prisoners in different compounds. Nevertheless, we soon found that these other 'privileged' Jews received better treatment; some did not have to do forced labour. Some did not have the *Appell* (roll call) and most received more food. On the other hand, there were other camps within the overall layout of Bergen-Belsen, where the treatment was reputed to be very much worse than in our Star Camp. In addition to the barbed wire fences, there was jute sacking or straw between the wires for isolation, so that we should not see the people in the other compounds, or what was happening there.

There were about a dozen barracks in the Star Camp and my father, Ruzzi and I were assigned to Barracks 11, one of the three extra-large brick-built barracks in Bergen-Belsen at the very end of our camp section. The barracks was almost 300 feet long and 60 feet wide, accommodating more than 400 inmates, and it was partitioned into several sections. We lived in Section D, together with 60-80 other male Jews from Holland. We slept in wooden three-tiered bunk beds. Several rows were pushed against each other, so we had to crawl across other peoples' bunks to get to our positions. I cannot remember the barracks number for my mother and Eve, but all the other barracks were of smaller size than ours, and built from wood and less resistant to the wind, rain and snow. Throughout, conditions were more primitive than in Westerbork, in terms of warmth, cleanliness and sanitation.

By the summer of 1944, more than 4,000 people were living in the Star Camp, all designated as 'exchange' Jews. The vast majority came from Holland and they were the most influential group in the Star Camp. But there were also Jews from Salonika in Greece, from the Drancy camp in France, and from several other countries. Everyone tended to speak their own language. We spoke Dutch, which was the dominant language in the Star Camp, and we roamed around with other boys of our age.

We were part of another strange paradox. The Nazis hated the Jews and wanted to kill them all in accordance with the Final Solution. At the same time, England and America were the principal enemies of the German Army. Yet the combination of English and American Jews were treated with respect and afforded special privileges!

The daily routine in the Star Camp started very early each morning (including Saturdays and Sundays) with the *Appell*. We had to line up in rows of five on the *Appellplatz* (parade ground) to be counted. This appears to have been a standard procedure in all the camps, and perhaps it was justified in those camps where escape was possible. But in our case the *Appell* was considered degrading, shameful and humiliating. Of more concern, in my opinion, were the potential medical problems arising from the long hours of standing in the rain and cold in extreme weather conditions.

The counting was done by senior prisoners who received minor privileges for enforcing the SS rules and commands. More often than not the count would not tally with the official SS figures, not because anyone had escaped, but because some people were ill and could not get out of their bunk. Others were in the camp hospital. Mothers with young children under three years old were excused from *Appell*, some people had died during the night, and others were out on special work details. All these people had to be counted separately in order to get the overall count correct and this would take two or three hours, and occasionally it could take all day. Meanwhile, we would stand out there in line, in the heat of the summer and in the freezing cold of the winter, in the biting wind and in pouring rain, sometimes in deep snow and often in the mud. The *Appellplatz* was an open field, without protection from the wind blowing across the heathland and we did not have much winter clothing. We had to stand all the time, and it was difficult just keeping our feet from freezing. The Germans did not care how long we stayed there.

I was back at Belsen in April 1987, when there was snow and slush on the ground, and even with a heavy overcoat, I felt the icy wind go right through me. I don't know how we survived the winter of 1944/45 with the minimal clothing at our disposal but I assume we just got used to it.

When everyone was accounted for, the senior prisoners would call the Jewish elders and the SS authorities, to verify the count against the official figures. After *Appell*, we returned to our barracks for our first 'meal' of the day. The five of us were able to take our meals together as a family, in this case a mug of warm brown water called *Ersatz Kaffee* (substitute coffee). Then the adults went off to work. We met together again for the other two 'meals', which consisted of a bowl of turnip soup at lunchtime and a one-and-a-half inch slice of black bread in the evening, with an occasional piece of sausage, cheese or jam. Three times each day we had to stand in line to receive these meagre rations. This was our diet for more than a year. Families in the Star Camp usually got together for their 'meals', but there was never any real privacy in the barracks. How did we survive? Especially the adults who had to work all day?

My father worked in the shoe tent, where they had to disassemble mountains of old shoes and boots in order to separate the leather parts for salvage. Apparently it was a very dirty and difficult job, for which my father and other 'intellectuals' were

totally unsuited, especially as they worked under the supervision
of a particularly nasty SS guard. I think my mother worked in the
kitchens, peeling potatoes or cleaning vegetables, which offered
opportunities for extra scraps of food. Some of the bread was
baked within the kitchens, whilst additional loaves were
transported from nearby towns. For some reason rations were the
same for adults and children, healthy and sick, workers and non-
workers. This may not have been fair, because it benefited
children who did not have to work; but many parents may have
wished it this way.

For some most fortunate reason, I did not have to work in
Bergen-Belsen, although the age limit was 15 and I was several
months older. As a rule, children of 14 and below lived with their
mothers in the female barracks and did not have to work. My
brother Ruzzi was only 12 years old on arrival, yet he lived with
my father and myself in a male barracks, but as we shall see later,
Ruzzi himself had arranged this!

The leader of the Star Camp – *Lagerältester* – was a Greek Jew
named Jacques Albala, and his deputy was Josef Weiss from
Holland. They headed a *Judenrat*, a Jewish Council, within the
camp just as in Amsterdam and Westerbork. We noted that the
first arrivals in the camp usually got the best jobs in the camp
hierarchy, both in Westerbork and in the Star Camp. Our
Blockältester (barracks elder) was called Pinner, also from Holland.
One of the few other names from Belsen that we remember is *Rooie*
(Red) Muller, an SS guard with ginger hair, who was in charge of
the sewers and drains and could often be seen in our camp with his
Jewish assistants. Two other men from our Star Camp worked in
the crematorium where they burned the bodies of inmates who had
died in the camp; another one worked as a barber, who also

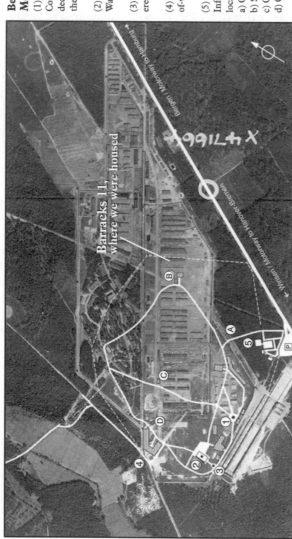

Bergen-Belsen Memorial Map

(1) Jewish Memorial (1946) Commemorative Stone dedicated by the President of the State of Israel (1987)

(2) Obelisk and Memorial Wall

(3) Wooden Cross (originally erected in 1945)

(4) Path to Soviet prisoner-of-war cemetery

(5) Document Centre Information points at key locations of the former camps
a) Camp boundary
b) Square for roll calls
c) Camp road
d) Crematoria

Mass Graves

Walkways for visitors

0 50 100 150 200 m

Barracks 11, where we were housed

The superimposed air photograph by the Royal Air Force shows the POW and concentration camp Bergen-Belsen on 13 September 1944. Used with kind permission of the Bergen-Belsen Documentation Centre.   Source: Air Photo Library, University of Keele, Great Britain.

attended to the SS. In this way we were able to find out what was happening in the outside world.

Children were also involved in the running of the camp. For example, Ruzzi was extremely enterprising and resourceful and he helped with the distribution of food for the 60 to 80 people in our section of the barracks. This job involved collecting food from the kitchens across the main road. It meant leaving the barbed wire fences of our camp and entering the barbed wire fencing surrounding the kitchens. The coffee and soup were transported in large urns and carried by two people. Individual portions were then dished out with a ladle. The soup presented particular opportunities for cheating, because the few nourishing potatoes and turnips were at the bottom of the urn, and even the demand for thorough stirring could not prevent the best parts of the soup going to the friends and relatives of the person in charge of dishing out the soup. Ruzzi was in charge of dishing out the soup in our barracks and on several occasions he was caught in unfair practices. He was sentenced by the Jewish Council to two or three days of solitary confinement in a bunker. Ruzzi accepted this as a hazard that went with the job and always returned to the same activities, with the same results. Presumably someone else would be doing the same fiddles, and maybe worse. There were similar opportunities for cheating with the bread rations. Officially, each large black bread loaf was to be divided into eight equal rations. This alone was difficult and some rations would be larger than others. My father, Ruzzi and I could ask for our rations to remain in one three-ration piece, thus avoiding the loss of bread due to slicing. Furthermore, we could return this piece next day (maybe after shaving off a millimetre) and exchange it for a six-ration piece. Ruzzi would retrieve all the crumbs. All in all, Ruzzi found plenty of opportunities for his initiative, which also added to the excitement of life in the camp. Ruzzi had noticed that in Westerbork during the day there were far fewer people in the men's barracks than in the women's barracks. Most children lived in the women's barracks and many adult women with children did not have to work. Therefore, when we arrived in Bergen-Belsen, Ruzzi opted to live with me and my father in the men's barracks – rather than with my mother and Eve in the women's as he had done at Westerbork. This would give him more chance of helping with the food distribution, which was almost a life and death opportunity. I regret to admit that many decent people were fighting over scraps of food. There was no shame attached to 'organising' food, clothing or anything else.

Our life in Bergen-Belsen, especially during 1944, was pretty dull, tedious and monotonous. Apart from the *Appell* and the meals, there was absolutely nothing to do for the children in the Star Camp. Some of our time was spent guarding our possessions, and any of our laundry hanging out to dry inside the barracks, because there was a certain amount of opportunistic theft in all the barracks. Any education was officially prohibited, and there was a lack of teaching and reading materials. Nevertheless, there were some secret impromptu school lessons and also attempts at religious education in individual barracks, conducted primarily by the over-65s and young mothers, who did not have to work during the daytime. One of the children would stand by the door and warn the teachers when any officials approached. There were also occasional birthday celebrations and other events to relieve the boredom.

The hard work during the day and the minimal food rations, not to mention the lack of facilities and equipment, made any structured teaching by adults extremely difficult, as well as dangerous. But daily religious services certainly did take place in our barracks. Many orthodox Jews prayed before and after the meals, and the major Jewish festivals were celebrated in most barracks. This was facilitated by books, stationery, religious artefacts etc., which we had brought from Amsterdam and Westerbork in our suitcases. The children, such as Ruzzi and me, learnt a lot from these services, perhaps because there wasn't anything else to learn. Our present *Haggadah* textbook for Passover mentions the Passover service conducted by the Jewish inmates of the German concentration camp at Bergen-Belsen in 1944 and the rabbis' decision to permit the eating of leavened bread. This may well have been in our Star Camp, but I cannot actually recall this event. However, I realise now that I knew almost nothing about Judaism at the beginning of the war, whereas by the end of the war, I could read Hebrew, recite most of the prayers, knew all the major festivals and could sing (very badly) many of the associated Hebrew songs. I must have learned all this in Amsterdam, Westerbork and Bergen-Belsen. After the war, I had another spell of 20 years without religion, until I got married and we started a family.

In addition to the absence of education, there was no opportunity for sports or athletics in Bergen-Belsen, because there was no equipment, not even a football. In fact, there were almost no facilities at all. There was cold running water for washing in the wash barracks, but no soap and no toothpaste of course. There were occasional communal showers, there were latrine barracks, with open ditches for toilets, and there was plenty of dirt and mud. The sanitary conditions were simply atrocious. I do not remember much heating inside the barracks and there certainly was no evening entertainment, as there was in Westerbork. There were also regular air-raid alarms, when we had to stay in our barracks and the lights were switched off. In addition, there was a curfew at night, when we were not allowed out of our barracks.

Later, when the typhus epidemic started, we spent many hours each day hunting the lice. They were everywhere: in the barracks, in the bunk beds and on our bodies, especially in our hair, and in our clothing. We had special wooden toothcombs to scrape the lice out of our hair. They liked to settle in the internal seams of our clothes, which meant that we had to take our clothes off, turn them inside out and then find the lice and squash them to death individually. Lice-hunting became a major occupation. It was almost fun for us youngsters, but it was a vital daily routine, as the lice were responsible for transmitting the typhus, which was contagious. Typhus fever would kill all but the strongest and fittest human beings. Unfortunately, the lice would lay eggs in any warm places on our bodies and thus the lice would multiply faster than we could kill them and we never managed to get rid of them. It was horrible to feel them crawling over your body and inside your clothes. We had occasional hot showers supposedly to kill the lice, but the heat did not kill the eggs and possibly even accelerated their growth.

We were never in physical danger inside the Star Camp. There was no shooting and no unwarranted beating in our compound. However, we lived in deteriorating squalor and misery, which is difficult to describe. We were slowly starving to death – although we may not have realised this at the time. We resigned ourselves to our fate, whatever that might be, although we never thought that we might die at that point. None of our contemporaries had died thus far. In some ways we were eternal optimists, because we always hoped and expected to be liberated and to survive this unfortunate period of our life. We longed to be back in Heemstede or in London. Thus, I celebrated my 16th birthday in captivity.

Of course, there were occasional times of excitement, such as the two exchanges to freedom of colleagues from the Star Camp that really happened. The first exchange took place in June 1944 and involved 222 Jews with entry visas for Palestine, including the Mainz family, who had lived across the road from us in Heemstede. Apparently there were some 1,000 Jewish inmates in the Star Camp with Palestine visas and the list was gradually whittled down, accompanied by overwhelming disappointment for many hopeful candidates. There was a last-minute panic when a member of a family of five persons selected for the exchange fell ill, and the Germans invited another family of five to take their place. My parents volunteered immediately, contrary to the rules of never volunteering and never wanting to go elsewhere, which might be worse (and there were people who doubted the reality of these exchange programmes), but we were not accepted, probably because we did not possess the actual Palestine visas. It was a major disappointment for our family, especially when we later heard that these 222 fortunate people really did get to Palestine within one month. They were exchanged against German 'Templers' from the Temple Society in Palestine – an orthodox Lutheran sect living near Jerusalem. There is a rumour that some of these 'Templers' were subsequently killed, when their train happened to be bombed by Allied planes in Germany.

The second exchange from the Star Camp happened very much later, in January 1945, involving more than 100 American Jews, and Jews with visas for South America. They were handed over to the International Red Cross and loaded onto a train heading towards Switzerland. We found out after the war, that they also reached their destination. One of these exchangees reported our presence in Bergen-Belsen to family friends abroad. It was rumoured that the exchange was based on five Germans for each American Jew, and that the British refused to exchange on this basis. In fact, there were very few British nationals in the Star Camp. I am aware of only two others, besides my sister Eve. These exchanges were obviously very important for the morale of the 'exchange' Jews and helped us enormously in maintaining hope and keeping our spirits up.

The British and American nationals were supposed to receive occasional parcels from the International Red Cross with food and clothing. However, there were considerable difficulties in distributing these parcels to the rightful owners. We did receive two such parcels, possibly sent by Aunt Liesl from Palestine. The parcels, which contained chocolate and other goodies, arrived in the spring of 1945. We were already in a very bad physical condition and could not digest such rich food, but of course we devoured everything. Some people may even have died from eating the Red Cross food. Nevertheless, the parcels were most welcome as a distraction and as an acknowledgement that our relatives knew where we were and continued to support us.

By this time, life in Bergen-Belsen was getting very much worse and we looked back to our time in Westerbork with nostalgia. During the autumn of 1944, the major concentration camps in the east, including Auschwitz, were being evacuated and the surviving inmates were transported or sent on 'death marches' to the camps in the west, such as Bergen-Belsen. Approximately 8,000 Jewish women from Auschwitz arrived in Bergen-Belsen in October/November 1944. They were housed in tents which were subsequently blown down during a major storm. In December 1944, the commandant of Auschwitz, SS *Hauptsturmführer* Josef Kramer, became the new commandant of Bergen-Belsen and it was designated as an official concentration camp with 15,000 inmates at that time. Kramer also brought his team of SS personnel from Auschwitz, including the notorious Irma Grese.

Whilst conditions deteriorated to real concentration camp standards, the 'exchange' Jews continued to receive 'privileged' treatment, but we were not able to speak to the women from Auschwitz or the other inmates in different compounds, from whom we were separated by barbed wire.

Another 80,000 prisoners would be transferred to Bergen-Belsen during the last four or five months of the war, causing severe overcrowding. These poor people were already in a terrible state when they arrived. There was no room for them and there was little food for them – and then the diseases and epidemics started. These culminated in the terrible scenes of ultimate hell, to be witnessed when Bergen-Belsen was eventually liberated by the British Army on Sunday 15 April 1945

Jewish prisoners totalling 34,000 died in Bergen-Belsen of starvation, exhaustion, neglect and disease during the last three months before the liberation. Another 13,000 died after the liberation. Even the British medical teams were unable to save them. In addition to the 50,000 Russian POWs, a total of almost 50,000 victims, mostly Jews, died in Bergen-Belsen. Not many, in the context of the six million Jews who perished in the Holocaust, but nevertheless equivalent to the entire population of a small town, and the way they died of starvation and disease is beyond imagination.

Meanwhile, during the winter of 1944/45, life was also getting worse for us privileged 'exchange' Jews in the Star Camp. Some of the barracks in the Star Camp were allocated to newcomers from the east, causing overcrowding. After almost a whole year on minimal food rations, we were becoming thin skeletons, severely under-nourished and always hungry. Worse, we lost our strength and resistance to illness and infection. We experienced diarrhoea and dysentery, making us weaker and liable to transfer to the so-called hospital barracks. The hygienic conditions were deplorable and there was no medicine. Few people came out of the hospital alive. As people in the Star Camp started to die, a general atmosphere of fear and mistrust developed. People were becoming more and more desperate. For example, we used some of the wooden slats from our bunk beds to light fires outside our barracks to cook scraps of food, such as potato peelings.

My mother became ill at this point and was transferred to the hospital barracks. We went to visit her every evening, but there was nothing we could do for her. There were no medicines, there was no extra food. One evening when we arrived, my mother had gone. Her body had already been removed to make way for another patient. She had died of starvation, sickness and exhaustion. It was 17 January 1945, just six days before her 43rd birthday. She had been so kind, friendly and intelligent, but she never had much opportunity to utilise all her talents. We realised later that we never really said 'goodbye' to my mother. But how could we? At the end of each visit, we just said, "See you tomorrow evening!" and hoped that we would.

Needless to say, we were heartbroken. We had lost a wonderful mother, a person who had never harmed a soul. It was the first death in our family that we were aware of. We did not know it at that time, but our four grandparents had already been murdered in

FINAL DESTINATION

Sobibor. We struggled on, like everyone else in the Star Camp. Many of our friends had similar experiences, and we got used to seeing dead people. With all the dead bodies lying around, we became quite tough, thick-skinned and resilient. It may sound callous now, but that is how it was. There was no point feeling sorry for ourselves; we had to be strong to survive. Eve was eight years old and most affected by the loss of her mother. They had always been together in the camps, and now she was alone in her barracks. She was very frightened, confused and utterly miserable. Fortunately there was a couple with visas for Palestine, Mr and Mrs Birnbaum, who had six young children of their own, and they offered to look after Eve. We remember them well. They were very orthodox Jews and we learned many of the Jewish prayers and songs from them. Eventually, they accumulated about 50 little orphan children within their 'orphanage' in Bergen-Belsen. Children seemed to survive better than adults. Perhaps they needed less food. They did not have to work and maybe parents diverted some of their meagre rations to their children.

By this time, the first quarter of 1945, the Allies had landed in Normandy and were well on their way through France, Belgium and Holland towards Germany itself. We could see large formations of Allied bombers flying overhead; at first only the British at night, but later also the Americans during the day, when we could admire the vapour trails high up in the sky. Occasionally, German fighters would attack the bombers and we could see planes being shot down. We sensed that the end of the war was near, and this helped to boost our morale.

But then, my father fell ill and was transferred to the hospital barracks, just like my mother had been two months earlier. I don't know whether it was typhus or dysentery, or just malnutrition, but he died in the hospital on 20 March 1945 at the age of 43. Apparently it was a common phenomenon in the camps, that husbands and wives often followed each other within a very short period of time. Perhaps they lost the will to live alone without their partner. In this way, dozens of children in the Star Camp became orphans in the early months of 1945. Today I am already 25 years older than my parents were when they perished in Bergen-Belsen. Now I can begin to understand how they must have felt at that time. I can imagine myself in their situation, dying in a concentration camp in front of our three young children. What a nightmare....

My father had always been respected and admired within the community. He had been a devoted husband and loving father. Another distinguished scholar and successful career destroyed, another life unfulfilled.... It was so, so sad for us. Again, we had failed to say goodbye. He had survived in the camps for almost two years. Just one more month, and Bergen-Belsen would be liberated. If the Allies could have finished the war just a few months earlier, both my parents – and many tens of thousands of other prisoners – might have been saved. Many camp survivors and historians have questioned the specific objectives of the Allied armies in relation to the German concentration camps. If the Russian Army had reached Auschwitz earlier; if the American Army had reached Buchenwald earlier; if the British Army had reached Bergen-Belsen earlier; hundreds and thousands of lives might have been saved – including my parents. Anne Frank died in Bergen-Belsen at that time in March 1945. As in Amsterdam, our paths crossed, but she was in the next section of the camp and again, we did not meet. My recent association with the 'Anne Frank in the World' exhibition has revealed the similarities in our stories.

FINAL DESTINATION

Now Eve, Ruzzi and I were orphans aged 8, 13 and 16. It was a cruel blow, but I do not believe that we appreciated all the implications at that time, except that there was no one to look after us and no one to turn to in case of difficulties. We did not even wonder how we would get on without parents after the war. In our anguish and misery we probably did very little thinking at that time. All three of us just instinctively got on with surviving, as best as we could. Unconsciously, we never despaired or gave up hope of survival. Death was for other older people, not for us youngsters. In retrospect, this was probably the worst time of my life; when we lost both our parents and we were all alone in Belsen during the worst days.

Ruzzi and I had to tend for ourselves during the last few weeks in Bergen-Belsen, as the general situation got worse and worse. There were more than 40,000 people in the camp and 600 were dying every day. In the early days, the dead bodies were placed into individual wooden coffins and transported by their surviving relatives and friends to the gate of our compound on a cart. From there, other prisoners hauled the cart to the crematorium. Later, there were insufficient coffins and eventually we were too weak and exhausted to carry the dead bodies to the camp gate. As the mortality rate kept rising, the corpses were piled high in front of the barracks. People were dying everywhere, even in the Star Camp.

By the beginning of April, we could actually hear the rumbling of the advancing Allied artillery in the distance and we became very excited at the prospect of liberation and freedom. Without our parents and without a home, where would we go, what would we do? The optimism and hope that we had always shared with our parents had disappeared. Instead I began to worry. Perhaps it was the responsibility for my younger brother and sister.

FROM BELSEN TO BUCKINGHAM PALACE

Suddenly, on 9 April 1945, the Star Camp was evacuated. We had a special shower session some days previously and our clothes were deloused, but we did not realise the significance. All inhabitants were assembled on the *Appellplatz* and those who could still walk were marched to the railway siding near Bergen. Fortunately, it was a beautiful sunny spring day, and we could collect and carry our remaining luggage and clothing, although most people did not have much left. We formed a group with other boys, who had also lost their parents in Bergen-Belsen. It took quite a long time to walk the few miles to the railway ramp, because most people were in very poor physical condition. The younger boys, such as Ruzzi, were probably the fittest and the liveliest. We were closely guarded at all times, with a certain amount of shouting and pushing, because even the guards were becoming nervous, as the British Army approached.

A total of about 7,000 'exchange' Jews from the Hungarian camp and the Star Camp were being evacuated and three trains were waiting for us. It was a mixture of third-class passenger coaches and cattle wagons. Most of the 'exchange' Jews from the Star Camp, including Ruzzi and myself, and the Birnbaums with Eve and other orphans, were allocated to the third train. As orphans, we were allowed to travel in one of the passenger coaches, although the Birnbaums appear to have chosen a cattle wagon, which enabled the young children to lie on the floor and sleep.

This was the only occasion, during the entire war, when I witnessed a deliberate shooting. While waiting at the railway siding, a young man ran off into the fields, but the guards spotted him and an SS officer called for a sharp-shooter. He came over, quite near to us, took aim and fired. Although the escaper was some distance away, he fell to the ground in the fields and the guards later recovered his body. Soon afterwards, we entered the train. I remember that we occupied a window seat, put our possessions in the overhead baggage nets and waited for the next move in this extraordinary situation. Where were we going and what would happen to us? Presumably the Nazis still hoped to exchange us or use us as hostages in impending truce negotiations.

How is it that I survived in Bergen-Belsen? I cannot claim that I actually did anything heroic or special in order to survive. I just did as I was told. I took no risks, and I never volunteered for anything. I kept a low profile. Ruzzi, on the other hand, was proactive. He 'organised', cheated and did anything he could – and sometimes could not – get away with. To some extent Ruzzi probably helped me to survive – and the Birnbaums certainly helped Eve to survive. In the same way, many inmates survived in pairs; mother and daughter, father and son, brother and sister, but I should add that we were fortunate to be 'exchange' Jews. More than half of the inmates of the Star Camp survived, especially the children.

JOURNEY TO NOWHERE
The last train, 9 April – 23 April 1945

The other two trains had departed, one of them with the remnants of the Hungarian camp, but we stayed in our train at the Bergen railway siding for another night, with about 2,500 other 'exchange' Jews from the Star Camp, mainly children. We were not allowed to leave the train. There was no food, no water, no toilets, no medicines; but there were SS guards. It was only on the afternoon of the next day, 10 April 1945, that we finally left Bergen in a northerly direction towards an unknown destination. On that day, the British Army, as it turned out, was only 25 miles away.

Just five days later, on Sunday 15 April 1945, the camp would be liberated by the British Army and the world would hear the famous broadcast by Richard Dimbleby and see the macabre photographs taken by the army and press photographers. 'Belsen' would become infamous overnight, synonymous with 'Man's inhumanity to Man', and remain so for decades, alongside

FROM BELSEN TO BUCKINGHAM PALACE

Auschwitz and Hiroshima, metaphors of our age. The camp commandant, Josef Kramer, would be described as the 'Beast of Belsen' and his team of SS guards would be tried in Lüneburg. Surprisingly, the name of 'Red' Muller was not among the list of 45 accused SS personnel. Perhaps he escaped. Eleven of the accused, including Kramer and Grese, would be sentenced to death by hanging, for their crimes committed in Auschwitz as well as Bergen-Belsen. Flame-throwers would be used to raze Bergen-Belsen to the ground in order to prevent the typhus epidemic from spreading. The nearby military barracks in Hohne would become the Bergen-Belsen Displaced Persons Camp for another five years, and the 13,000 post-liberation victims from the camp would be buried within the military camp area.

Also on 15 April 1945, President Roosevelt would be buried. He had died on 12 April 1945 and just failed to see the end of the war in Europe, which he had prosecuted so successfully alongside Churchill and Stalin.

But we missed it all! We had been in Bergen-Belsen for 434 days, but we were not there for the liberation. By that time, on 15 April, our 'Last Train' (sometimes referred to as the 'Phantom Train' or 'The Lost Transport' by other survivors of this train journey) was near Lüneburg, just south of Hamburg, travelling east and waiting to cross the river Elbe. Apparently there was only one remaining railway bridge over the Elbe and the Germans were ready to blow it up before the British Army arrived. Our train crossed the bridge and the bridge was destroyed.

After leaving the Bergen siding, the train stopped in the station at Soltau, where we caught up with the Hungarian train and met other trainloads of refugees going in the opposite direction. There was a lot of confusion but we managed to obtain some food, in exchange for jewellery left by our parents. There was also an air raid while we were in Soltau. Eventually we moved on, and when we reached Lüneburg, we had travelled about 60 miles in five days. This established the pattern of our train journey. We would move sufficiently far away from the advancing Allied armies, not to be captured by them. Our train was subjected to Allied strafing, despite the white sheets hanging out of our windows and draped on the roof of the train. The Germans had attached some military equipment to the back of the train, hence the persistent air attacks. I particularly remember one series of attacks by two Allied fighter planes, with distinctive twin fuselages – American Lockheed P-38 Lightnings. We all rushed out of the train and ran into the fields and watched the spectacle from a safe distance, lying flat against the ground in the fields. Having made several low level passes over the train, they then disappeared over the horizon as quickly as they arrived. The fires that were started on the train were soon put out and the train managed to continue its journey.

Before we returned to the train, we collected anything edible from the fields, including grass. Ruzzi and his friends lit a fire on the platform at the end of our coach, using the planks from the seats as firewood. The Germans always tended to plant potatoes along the railway lines, which turned out to be very convenient for us starving passengers. It was a delicious meal and every time the train stopped, we all wandered into the fields to collect food and firewood. The SS guards had become less fanatical and seemed to have lost interest in us. Perhaps they were more concerned about their own future. To avoid attacks from the air, the train tended to move only at night. During the day, it was parked in woods and forests, out of sight of Allied planes. As we became used to the new routines, we ventured further and further during the daylight hours, and the engine driver would whistle for us to return to the train before setting off. We even entered nearby villages and begged and bartered and stole real food: bread and butter and milk and fruit. We took these luxuries back to the train and devoured them eagerly.

One day in 1991, as I was telling this story to the members of a local Rotary club, one war veteran asked: "Why did you go back to the train?" I was quite flabbergasted, and it took me some time to respond. Escape was something that we never ever thought about. Not during our train journey and not at any time in Bergen-Belsen nor in Westerbork. Now that I have seen films about 'Colditz', 'The Wooden Horse' and 'The Great Escape', I wonder what we missed. However, POWs were trained to escape, in fact it was their duty to attempt to escape. We were never at any time told by our parents, or by our leaders or 'elders' in the camp, that we should try to escape. In fact, the opposite was true, because any attempt might have led to vicious reprisals, often involving innocent bystanders. But it remains an interesting proposition. We certainly could have chosen not to go back to the train very easily. However, we would have been left stranded among the German population, who might have reported these suspicious characters to the Gestapo and we would have been shot. On the other hand, we might have survived in the woods and fields until the British Army arrived. Hopefully they would have recognised us as prisoners among the thousands of German refugees milling around. But that is all speculation ....

Anyway, we always returned to the train from our excursions, and we are not aware of any colleagues that used the opportunity to escape. In many ways, we had become a community that stuck together. The fact that people from our train were dying of starvation and disease every day, and that we buried them by the side of the railway track, also helped to foster a spirit of camaraderie among us.

We progressed in an easterly direction, through Wittenberg by the Elbe and to Berlin itself: the capital of Germany and my birthplace. We traversed the entire city from northwest to southeast on 19 April 1945, passing our home area of Tempelhof, just two weeks before the Russian Army arrived. We could see the terrible devastation caused by the Allied bombing. Whole areas of the city were in ruins, and not a single house was left undamaged. I do not believe any one of us felt much pity for the German population. We did not see much of them, so perhaps they lived permanently in their air-raid shelters, or were preparing for the arrival of the Russians. Maybe they had joined the long lines of refugees fleeing on foot with their possessions. However, we did pass a few military trains with anti-aircraft guns, manned by young boys from the Hitler Youth. They were obviously going to defend Berlin from the Russian Army. We were beginning to fancy our chances of survival better than theirs.

Having left Bergen-Belsen in a northerly direction, then heading east, the train now turned south, travelling between the British and American Armies on one side and the Russian Army on the other. The Germans were still keeping us for exchange or hostage purposes. In 1943, Hitler had ordered that the 'exchange' Jews should be held as hostages, to be exchanged for German nationals in other countries. Joseph Kramer was obviously unwilling to disobey the Führer's orders, and so ordered the evacuation of the three trains so that we could continue as potential hostages.

FROM BELSEN TO BUCKINGHAM PALACE

It is interesting that the first of the three trains from Bergen-Belsen apparently set off in the direction of the Theresienstadt camp near Prague. Theresienstadt has always been regarded as a model camp and it is quite likely that this was meant to be the destination for all three trains. But the first train never reached Theresienstadt. It was liberated by an advance unit of the American Army at Farsleben, near Magdeburg, just a few days after leaving Bergen-Belsen. Apparently there were 400 'exchange' Jews from the Star Camp among the 2,500 passengers on this first train. I have never found out what happened to the second train and its passengers, but some historians claim that this train did reach Theresienstadt on 21 April. Anyway, we took a more northerly route, bypassing Magdeburg and thus avoiding capture by the American Army. Then the train turned southeast, roughly in the direction of Theresienstadt.

Of course, we did not know any of this in April 1945 as we journeyed slowly through the German countryside, frequently stopping to avoid air attacks. We had become used to our nomadic existence. The end came very suddenly. One evening, we went to sleep on the train as usual, and when we woke up next morning, there was a commotion outside. We could see Russian Cossack soldiers on horseback and found that our SS guards had disappeared during the night. It was 23 April 1945. We had been on the train for 14 days and 14 nights, and we were near a village in a forested area called Tröbitz (population 700) in eastern Germany. We had been liberated. It was as sudden and uneventful as that.

Two days later, on 25 April 1945, the Red Army would meet up with the American Army near Torgau on the river Elbe, just 20 miles away from us – and two weeks later, the war in Europe would be at an end.

LIBERATION

Alive but alone

Photo: Ruzzi (bottom right) and I with Mr and Mrs Birnbaum celebrating our first Shabbat
after liberation. Maastricht, 1945

ORGANISING OUR LIFE

Tröbitz, April – May 1945

Liberation was a massive anticlimax. There was no kissing, no laughing or singing or dancing or hand-shaking or embracing. We were not expecting to be liberated, and we were certainly not prepared. It was quite a new experience for us. Most of us had not been 'free' for five years, since the German invasion of Holland in May 1940, and we had been incarcerated for almost two years, since June 1943. We were in no mood, and in no condition, to celebrate. There were no carefree parties, there was no pleasure, no joy and no hilarity among any of us. Perhaps surprise, relief and excitement best describe our feelings when we realised that we had finally been liberated.

We were certainly not ready for the new situation. In Amsterdam, Westerbork, and Bergen-Belsen, we were always told what to do and what not to do! Then, we had our parents to supervise our activities. We soon found that freedom was not as easy as we had expected. First, we had to explain to the Russians who we were. We did not speak Russian, and they did not speak Dutch, and we did not dare to speak German, as they were liable to shoot Germans on the spot. Eventually we managed to convince the Russian officer that we had been prisoners of the Nazis and that we were on their side. We fixed badges of red, white and blue to our coats and jackets, instead of the yellow stars, which we quickly removed.

When we needed food, I wandered off into the fields to collect the usual potatoes and greens. In the evening, when Ruzzi and his friends came back from the nearby village with white bread, milk and honey, they laughed at me and told me to do better the next day. And I did. The next day I found a nearby cheese factory and I also found a wheelbarrow, so I returned to the train with a wheelbarrow full of tubes of cheese paste and was rightly proud of myself. Then Ruzzi and the others came back from Tröbitz with meat and fruit, gateaux and preserves from the cellars of German homes. They also had watches, cameras, bicycles and even cars, which they had commandeered from the Germans. Ruzzi was a first-class scavenger, quick-witted and streetwise, fearless and resourceful.

He acquired a motorcycle and also found a fur hat from a dead Russian Army officer, which he wore with pride during the months ahead. It would later cover his shaven head. The Germans were rightly scared of the Russians and we only needed to refer to the Russians, and the Germans would give us anything. We called it 'organising' and 'liberating'. In fact it was plundering and looting and, as we found out later, it happened everywhere during the last days of the war.

Many of the families from our train actually moved into the

German houses in Tröbitz, either with or without their German owners' approval. Many of the German inhabitants had fled from the advancing Russians.

Eventually, the Jewish survivors from the train more or less took over the town of Tröbitz and many families lived there for many months. The Jewish leaders established the usual Council of Elders, and even issued certificates to confirm survival in Bergen-Belsen and on the 'Last Train' for individual applicants, signed by Josef Weiss (deputy leader of the Star Camp) and Mr I. S. de Vries (a Dutch lawyer from Amsterdam).

I blame my pathetic performance and slow reactions on my poor state of health. My body, especially my legs, was very bloated and swollen, and I had some difficulty moving around. Apparently this condition is called 'oedema' and is caused by an excess of fluid in the tissues, in my case due to severe malnutrition. It is strange that the pictures of inmates from concentration camps always show thin, emaciated skeletons, and I have never seen anyone looking swollen and bloated, as I did in Tröbitz. I was in pretty poor shape and that is my excuse for not participating properly in the mass looting at the time of our liberation. My condition actually got worse, because within a few days of our liberation, both Ruzzi and I went down with typhus and we developed purple spots on our bodies – 'spotted fever'. We were lucky and were taken to a Russian Army hospital with excellent facilities near Riesa, where we were thoroughly cleaned and deloused, and all our hair shaved off. Two weeks later, the war in Europe ended, though we were not aware of any parties or other celebrations. We had a terrible fever and were delirious, but we were well looked after and we received good medical care. Although we survived, many others from our 'Last Train' died of typhus and over-eating and more than 500 of the 2,500 on the train were buried in a special Jewish cemetery in Tröbitz. In 1995, a Memorial Wall was dedicated in Tröbitz to their memory.

When we had recovered in the Riesa hospital, we asked to be repatriated to Holland, where we had lived before the war, where we had many friends and where our parents had left our belongings. There were many other survivors like us, and the Russians agreed to take all of us to Leipzig, which was in the American zone.

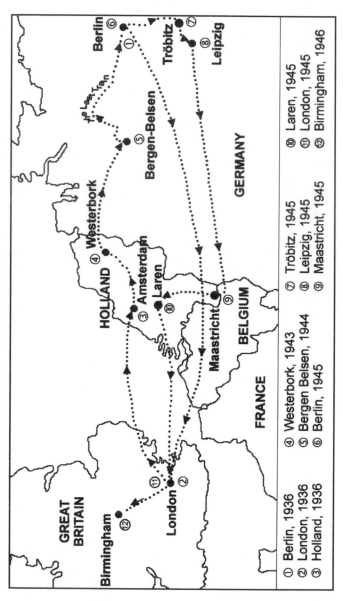

Map of my journey: 1936 – 1946

① Berlin, 1936   ④ Westerbork, 1943   ⑦ Tröbitz, 1945   ⑩ Laren, 1945
② London, 1936   ⑤ Bergen Belsen, 1944   ⑧ Leipzig, 1945   ⑪ London, 1945
③ Holland, 1936   ⑥ Berlin, 1945   ⑨ Maastricht, 1945   ⑫ Birmingham, 1946

AMERICAN INTERLUDE

Leipzig, May – June 1945

When we arrived in Leipzig in the American zone, together with many other Jewish survivors from Bergen-Belsen, we were confronted by sceptical military administrators, who wanted to know who we were and where we came from. At least we could communicate with the Americans in broken English, but we had almost no documents to prove our identity. The Russians had not even tried to interrogate us individually or record our names and background. At that time, in the chaotic aftermath of the Allied victory, there were tens of thousands of refugees wandering around Germany, including Germans whose homes had been destroyed. Soldiers from the *Wehrmacht* and even Nazis from the SS, who were pretending to be ordinary refugees were trying to slip through the net. It was obviously quite a difficult task for the Americans to sort it all out: who deserved food and attention and who should be imprisoned.

FROM BELSEN TO BUCKINGHAM PALACE

We told them our story and our group of Jewish survivors was then transferred to a military camp at Leipzig and we were accommodated in large multi-storey barracks. We slept on camp beds. We had chairs and tables in our rooms, and we received plenty of food (and chewing gum!) and some clothes from the Americans. I remember that one day we had a big fight with some of our room-mates, and we threw their possessions out of the window onto the parade ground. The Americans were not impressed. After further adventures, they eventually agreed to send us all back to Holland. Towards the end of June 1945, the Americans assembled a large convoy of several hundred Jewish camp survivors from Holland, Belgium and France, for repatriation by train to their home countries. We climbed onto open American Army trucks and just as we were leaving the camp, we stopped by the exit gate. Another open truck entered the camp with many children, younger than ourselves. Amongst them was our sister Eve! Ruzzi recognised her immediately and we shouted to stop the incoming truck. Eve was transferred to our truck and the three of us together were re-united and on our way back to Holland.

This was one of those extraordinary coincidences that occasionally happen in times of war. If our truck had left five minutes earlier, or if Eve's truck had arrived five minutes later, we might never have seen each other again – and Eve, our British-born sister, had been the principal reason why we were still alive. There is no doubt that without Eve, we would have been sent from Westerbork to Auschwitz or Sobibor in 1943, and our chances of survival there, at the ages of 11 and 14, would have been minimal. Ruzzi and I owe our survival in Bergen-Belsen to our special 'exchange' status, derived entirely from Eve's British birth certificate. Yet we had forgotten all about Eve after our departure from Bergen-Belsen on the 'Last Train'. We knew that she was on the same train, together with many other young children whose parents had died in Bergen-Belsen, in the makeshift orphanage of the Birnbaums. But during the two-week journey on the train and the subsequent days of liberation, we were busy looking after ourselves and, regretfully, we overlooked Eve's welfare. Then we had our time with typhus in the hospital. Afterwards, we looked for her, but we never found her. In fact, we understand that the Birnbaums and their orphans, including Eve, were accommodated in a large house in Tröbitz. We never found out what happened to her on the 'Last Train' and in Tröbitz, until our miraculous meeting in Leipzig. Eve was almost nine years old, and much affected by her experiences and does not remember anything about these events.

The Americans drove us to the Leipzig railway station and to our train – a long line of about 20 cattle wagons. The Americans did not appreciate the irony of the cattle wagons, but for us it evoked some very nasty memories from our time in Westerbork. We had seen exactly such trains at regular weekly intervals, destined for Auschwitz and Sobibor. But this time we were not packed in like sardines and the doors were not locked. All the sliding doors remained open throughout the journey; and the Americans gave us lots of food for the journey and we could take all our luggage and 'loot' with us. The train left Leipzig and made its way to the west. There were many stops and deviations as it was only six weeks after the end of the war, and the railway tracks had not yet been fully repaired after the bombings. We travelled through many German towns and cities and we could see the results of the Allied bombing. For example, our train came through the city of Kassel, an important railway junction, which was almost totally destroyed, but I do not remember any of us feeling sorry for the tremendous destruction.

In actual fact, we enjoyed our train ride through Germany, sitting in the doorway with our legs dangling outside. Many of us travelled on the roofs of the wagons, even jumping from one wagon roof to the next while the train was moving towards Holland. We even stayed on the roofs under bridges and in tunnels. It was pretty scary, but we were in a strangely euphoric mood. After all we had survived and the deaths that we had seen, life was cheap and we felt almost indestructible, even immortal.

'UN WELCOME HOME'
Maastricht, June 1945

On 28 June 1945, almost exactly two years after our deportation from Amsterdam to Westerbork on 20 June 1943, Eve, Ruzzi and I arrived at Maastricht on the southern tip of Holland, a town which nobody had heard of until a few years ago. All of the survivors destined for Holland left the train, which then continued its journey to repatriate the camp survivors from Belgium and France. Now we faced the Dutch authorities and the formalities of civilisation. First they took all our belongings away from us, including the motorcycle which Ruzzi had 'organised' in Tröbitz. Our clothes were disinfected and returned, but the motorcycle was not – the Dutch authorities did not approve of looting. Ruzzi was devastated. Then we were thoroughly scrubbed and cleaned, dusted with DDT and medically examined. Afterwards, the Dutch administrators took over and completed the Allied Expeditionary Force Displaced Persons Registration Record for each of us. I still have our original three Record Cards and the corresponding D. P. Index Cards. These would be our first official identity cards to show who we were and where we came from. My registration number was NG09045009. We had no other proof of our identity at that time. This was the occasion when I conveniently forgot the 'Friedrich' from my birth certificate. The card also shows that we came from Leipzig and that we had been 'Jewish prisoners in Bergen-Belsen'. We never had registration cards or work cards or bath cards like in Westerbork, and we had no tattooed numbers on our forearms as in Auschwitz.

Unfortunately, the Dutch official noted that Ruzzi and I were born in Berlin. He would not accept that the Nazis had cancelled our German citizenship and that we were stateless. He decided that we were Germans – and all Germans belonged in a camp. Accordingly, Ruzzi and I were sent to a nearby camp for 'enemy aliens' in Vaals, where we lived for several days with German inmates. These included captured SS officers, who appeared as nonchalant and arrogant as ever. This was not a very pleasant experience and not the sort of welcome we had expected in Holland. It cast a sinister shadow over the excitement of being back home in Holland. In fact, in all our years under Nazi rule in Germany, in Holland, and in the camps, I cannot remember ever being really frightened. We were never threatened with a gun or a truncheon, and we were never kicked or beaten. But now in Vaals, locked up with German soldiers and SS officers and maybe former Gestapo officials, I was terrified. It must have been obvious to them that we were Jewish survivors from the concentration camps. Fortunately, they were probably more concerned with their own future and how they were going to avoid a long prison sentence, or worse – and they never even spoke to Ruzzi and me during those horrible few days in Vaals.

'UN-WELCOME HOME'

Of course, Eve had a copy of her birth certificate and she was recognised as British. The administrators contacted Tante Fie, our pre-war neighbour in Amsterdam and she came to fetch Eve immediately and looked after her at her home in the Vechtstraat in Amsterdam, in the apartment below the one we had lived in two years earlier.

We also communicated with various Dutch friends and colleagues of our parents, who managed to vouch for us, and after four days, on 2 July 1945, we were released from Vaals and allowed to travel to the *Bergstichting* Jewish Orphanage, not too far from Amsterdam, where Eve was staying with Tante Fie. It was in Laren, not far from Naarden, where we had lived in 1941.

The first post-war photograph of Ruzzi and myself was taken in Maastricht, together with Mr and Mrs Birnbaum, their eldest daughter and another boy survivor from Belsen. Ruzzi was wearing his Russian officer's fur hat in June, and I was also wearing a cap to hide my shaven head during the first Friday evening Kiddush ceremony after our return to Holland. Many years later, we found out that the Birnbaums emigrated to Nahariya in Israel, but they both died before we had a chance to visit them and to thank them for looking after Eve during those terrible months in 1945.

JUST WAITING
Laren, July – November 1945

Ruzzi and I soon established ourselves in the *Bergstichting* at No. 4 Doodweg (Death Way, how appropriate!), under the supervision of Mr and Mrs Cohen. We regularly went to visit the Haas family, pre-war friends of our parents in nearby Hilversum, and we went back to school in September. I actually returned to the Gooise HBS secondary school in Bussum, where I had passed the entrance examination four years earlier in June 1941. I had just celebrated my 17th birthday and I cannot remember which class I attended, but I had lost at least two full academic years while I was in the camps. Although I did not realise it at the time, I had also lost two years of my 'teens' and the attendant non-academic activities and pursuits.

One of our first tasks in Laren was to establish contact with our sole remaining relatives, our father's brother and sister, in England and Palestine, respectively. We wrote to Uncle Rudi and

FROM BELSEN TO BUCKINGHAM PALACE

Aunt Lotte in London in July. They had moved several times during the war however, and it took some time for our letter to reach them. They responded favourably and their first letter to us was dated 8 August. In mid-September, Uncle Rudi was able to visit us in Laren. He had been interned as an enemy alien at the beginning of the war, then joined the Pioneer Corps and finished his five years of military service in the Intelligence Corps, where his knowledge of German helped with the interrogation of prisoners of war. His military contacts enabled him to fly to Holland at short notice and we very much appreciated his visit. We had been fending for ourselves for six difficult months after the death of our parents, and we had adopted a strange lifestyle. We tended to rebel against authority and disapprove of rules and regulations. We were fortunate in having friends and relatives, as there were many other orphans who were simply all alone. Some may well have emigrated to Israel, after its independence was established in 1948, as the only place where they felt welcome and at home.

We went to see Eve in Amsterdam, and despite her desire to stay with Tante Fie, it seemed better for her to return to her family. As a British subject, she was able to accompany Uncle Rudi on his return flight to London. Thus Eve arrived in London in mid-September 1945 as one of the first of the very few British-born survivors of Belsen and the Holocaust. Unfortunately, Eve did not speak any English, nor German, only Dutch. Uncle Rudi and Aunt Lotte spoke English and German, but no Dutch! Without Ruzzi or myself to translate, this language barrier caused some early difficulties, and Eve was not very happy in London. She had been mollycoddled by Tante Fie, which was probably what she needed after her camp experiences when she arrived in England.

JUST WAITING

We also received a letter from Aunt Liesl in Jerusalem. She had married Dr Leo Schindel and they had two young children, Daniela and Oren. They invited us to come to Palestine where they would look after us. But by that time we had committed ourselves to Uncle Rudi and London, where we had lived in 1936. We were budding Anglophiles, to whom Palestine in 1945 looked rather less attractive. However, we remained thankful to Aunt Liesl and Uncle Leo for their kind offer of hospitality, and we have visited them on several occasions since. Unfortunately, they have also both passed away now. They would have been interested in reading our story.

We also contacted our parents' friends in Holland, and spent most of our free time at weekends visiting them. We told them what had happened to us and recovered our belongings, which our parents had left with them for safe-keeping during the war. Some of these good friends lived in Amsterdam, Bussum, Naarden and Wassenaar. It was most fortunate that we recovered such prized possessions as our Märklin electric train set, Leica camera, cutlery and jewellery, books, documents and photographs. The latter have been invaluable to remind me of many experiences in my life that I would otherwise have completely forgotten.

Meanwhile Uncle Rudi made arrangements for Ruzzi and me to come to England and he applied for our UK entry visas. Apparently there was a special Distressed Relatives' Scheme, for survivors of concentration camps who had relatives in Britain, who were willing and able to look after them. Uncle Rudi was demobbed in October 1945, after five years in the British Army. I eventually inherited his demob trilby hat!

We obtained our official Dutch 'Identity Certificate for Aliens' on 13 November 1945, and our UK entry visas were issued by the

FROM BELSEN TO BUCKINGHAM PALACE

British Embassy in The Hague on 21 November. Two days later, early on the morning of 23 November 1945, Ruzzi and I arrived by ferry in Harwich, together with a group of other camp survivors, who had also been fortunate in obtaining entry visas to Britain. We took the train to London and had porridge and kippers for breakfast. For some unexplained reason, I have never eaten any kind of fish since that day. I was wearing 'plus fours' trousers, quite fashionable in Holland at the time, but only worn by golfers and eccentrics in England. We arrived at Liverpool Street Station, where we were met by Uncle Rudi – exactly seven months after we had been liberated by the Red Army near Tröbitz. All the excitement was effectively over. Now we would start a new life and try to forget all about the Nazis and Belsen.

I was just 17 years old, perhaps rather naïve and not aware of all the difficulties that still lay ahead.

AFTER THE WAR

A second life

Photo: Corinne and I, Marston Green, 1963

PREPARING FOR A FUTURE
London, November 1945 – January 1947

Uncle Rudi and Aunt Lotte literally opened their doors for us. They lived in a ground-floor flat, within a block of 60 flats in Neville's Court, Dollis Hill near Cricklewood in northwest London, with their young son Peter and daughter Ruth. Adding Eve, Ruzzi and me to their family proved quite difficult, physically and financially, but they did it and nobody complained. They were our official guardians and we were their unofficial adopted children.

As far as I can remember, nobody asked us about our experiences during the war, and we were not anxious to remember all these horrible events. At that time in 1945/6, Belsen was a very high profile subject and it did not require any contributions from us to explain what had happened there.

I expressed an interest in engineering, in stark contrast to my father's academic and commercial career, and started work at the

Hendon Precision Engineering Co. in Marylebone Lane. There I worked from December 1945 until November 1946. I attended evening classes to gain university entrance qualifications and soon passed the matriculation examinations, although English was the most difficult subject for me.

We were introduced to Uncle Rudi and Aunt Lotte's circle of friends, mostly Jewish pre-war refugees from Germany like themselves. Together with their children, we went to the cinema to see *The Wizard of Oz* and to football matches at Fulham, travelling by bus and underground. Everything was a new experience for us. I went cycling on Uncle Rudi's bike, ice-skating at Wembley and we enjoyed visiting Lyons Corner House in the West End. We encountered very little Jewish education during this period, although Ruzzi and I both managed to complete our *Bar Mitzvah* ceremonies early in 1946 at the New Liberal Jewish Congregation in Buckland Crescent. The service was conducted by Rabbi Dr Salzberger and Oberkantor Davidsohn. The congregation was made up mainly of pre-war refugees from Germany and Austria, and was the forerunner of the present Belsize Square Synagogue.

Uncle Rudi was still in the clothing business, later managing a company in the West End of London, importing gloves. His varied interests ranged from art to music and languages. He was an ardent stamp collector and car enthusiast. Among his succession of cars was a black Austin A90 Atlantic, an early sports coupé with a third 'cyclops' central headlight. I remember that quite vividly. We also had a memorable day at London's Northolt Airport, where the whole family took a sightseeing trip over London in a DC3 Dakota – my first flight.

PREPARING FOR A FUTURE

However, Uncle Rudi and Aunt Lotte could not really cope with all three of us, and after 12 months in London, I went to Birmingham under the auspices of the Jewish Refugees Committee. At a later stage, Ruzzi and Eve also went on their separate ways and left Uncle Rudi and Aunt Lotte's comfortable home.

Despite our dispersion, Uncle Rudi and Aunt Lotte remained our surrogate parents and Neville's Court remained our family home, where we met for festivals and holidays. The reunion over the Christmas holiday period, with goose and home-made German *klösse* (dumplings), remained a family tradition even when Uncle Rudi and Aunt Lotte moved to Holly Lodge Gardens in Highgate.

Sadly Uncle Rudi passed away in 1994 at the age of 87, followed by Aunt Lotte in 1996 at the age of 89, after suffering from Parkinson's disease for more than five years. They were a devoted and inseparable couple. We were privileged to have been brought up by them and we are forever grateful to them both. Their deaths were preceded by the untimely passing away of their talented and hard-working daughter Ruth, who died of cancer in Edinburgh earlier in 1994 at the young age of 49. She had a distinguished career in a number of fields, and her tragic illness and premature death was a bitter blow to Uncle Rudi and Aunt Lotte and to all the family.

I shall always be grateful to Uncle Rudi and Aunt Lotte, and to the British authorities, for the opportunity to start a new life in England.

ALL WORK AND NO PLAY
Birmingham, January 1947 – January 1964

I arrived in Birmingham in January 1947, totally alone, with just one name as a contact from the Jewish Refugees Committee in London: Ruth Simmons (later Ruth Wolf, OBE). She turned out to be absolutely marvellous, although perhaps I did not appreciate this at the time. Ruth arranged my accommodation in a small Jewish hostel in Radnor Road, Handsworth, run by Mrs Müller, an elderly lady from Austria. There were several other pre-war refugees staying with her. Ruth also helped me to obtain a five-year apprenticeship with BSA Tools in Marston Green, Birmingham, which kept me occupied during the daytime from 1946 until 1951. In the evenings I attended the Birmingham Technical College in Suffolk Street, studying towards a London University external degree in mechanical engineering.

I enjoyed life in England and soon adapted to English manners and customs. I liked the English people and I hoped to live the rest of my life in England. I wanted to be British, although at this time my nationality was not at all clear.

I had been born in Berlin, but the Nazis took away my German citizenship and I became stateless. After the war, the anti-Jewish Nazi laws were repealed, and the Dutch authorities, in Maastricht in June 1945, decided that I was German again. I do have my Berlin birth certificate, but no German passport. Instead, the Dutch gave me an 'Identity Certificate for Aliens' in 1945, which stated that I was of German origin. In England, I first received an Identity Card, and in 1947 I obtained a Travel Document, which was like a passport and allowed me to travel throughout Europe, with appropriate visas, but did not mention my nationality. I probably could have applied for a German passport, but I certainly did not want to be a German again – after all that we had been through during the war. I soon spoke English fluently, even with a 'Brummie' accent, and fortunately without a trace of a German accent. I am particularly pleased about that, because I do not want to be mistaken for a German. In fact, it is now the other way round, and I speak German and Dutch with an English accent.

As soon as I had completed the obligatory five years' residence qualification in England, I applied to the Home Office for naturalisation, and in April 1951 I received my Certificate of Naturalisation. In May 1951, I obtained my first British passport, which I was most proud to flash at immigration officers, especially during my first visit to Germany.

"I see you were born in Berlin, so can we speak in German?" said the German passport official in German. "Pardon?" I replied in English.

It is interesting that my recent application for a German pension was refused, apparently because I was no longer a German citizen. I was advised to apply for a German passport and then my application for a German pension might be reconsidered. I have not bothered. I still do not want to become German again – not even with dual nationality. I do not like to speak German, especially not in Germany, except in emergencies such as when ordering meals! Nevertheless, like many German Jews, I have inherited certain German characteristics which will never change.

I passed my university entrance examinations and after seven years of evening study, graduated in mechanical engineering with first class honours in 1954. I subsequently gained a master's degree in thermodynamics at Birmingham University in 1955. This was my only full-time education since 1940, when I was 12 years old.

I became a chartered automobile engineer (CEng) within the Institution of Mechanical Engineers, and eventually a Fellow Member (FIMechE). I am proud of my academic and professional achievements, after the early difficulties and interruptions during the war.

In 1953, my brother Ruzzi and I returned to the site of the Belsen camp, travelling by motorcycle. It was the first time we had been back in Germany and it was not a pleasant experience. We spoke to very few Germans and did not feel particularly welcome at that time. The Belsen site was unrecognisable; absolutely nothing was left from the original camp. There was a plaque near the entrance and a primitive notice board, but no visitor entrance and no visitors. It was a chilling experience, in more ways than one. The nearby railway siding, two or three miles from Belsen, was still there, unchanged. By this time I had also visited the Yad Vashem Holocaust Memorial Museum in Jerusalem, but otherwise, I had forgotten all about the Holocaust and I had never talked about my experiences or met another camp survivor. Nobody asked me about Belsen and I did not think anyone was interested to hear about it or discuss the subject at that time.

I left Mrs Müller and lived in various places in Birmingham. Eventually, when I attended Birmingham University full time, Ruth Simmons arranged for me to live in Vernon Road, Edgbaston, in the flat of Mrs Bach, another elderly refugee lady from Europe. In 1958, I left BSA and joined Lucas, first in the Group Research Centre in Marston Green, and from 1961 at Lucas Girling in Tyseley, working in the engineering department on braking systems for passenger cars.

During all my time in Birmingham, I had rarely been near a synagogue. Ruth Simmons remedied this and introduced me to Rabbi Bernard Hooker and in 1960 I joined the Liberal Jewish Synagogue in Sheepcote Street.

CORINNE AND FAMILY
Solihull, January 1964 – January 1990

In January 1964 I bought my first home, a semi-detached house in Lyndon Road, Olton, ready for another big event. On 26 March 1964 I married Corinne Jeanette Orme, a nurse eight years younger than myself (to look after me in my old age). We had known each other for some years, from the Birmingham University Students Union Saturday night hops and subsequent parties. We had also seen each other at jazz clubs, notably the 'Adam and Eve' in Bradford Street. But I was always busy with sports, and later Corinne was working in London and the Isles of Scilly. Eventually I managed to track her down, and we married and settled in Olton, Solihull.

Corinne worked as a midwife, and later as ward sister in Solihull Hospital. She was studying for the Open University in the evenings and gained a degree in Social Sciences. At the same time Corinne converted and was admitted to the Jewish faith. In the meantime, she left nursing to become a teacher and was soon a lecturer in nursing studies at the Solihull College. In between all these activities, Nicholas (1965), Simon (1967) and Judith (1970) were born. In August 1968 we moved to a new house in Hansell Drive, Dorridge, and lived there happily for 25 years. Our children grew up in Dorridge and all attended Sunday morning *cheder* classes at the Birmingham Progressive Synagogue in Sheepcote Street. They accomplished their *Bar* and *Bat Mitzvah*, and looked forward to the annual *Kadimah* Jewish Progressive summer camps.

Although all three children spent some time in Israel, Judith maintained her strong interest in Judaism and eventually made *aliyah* immediately after her graduation from Leeds in 1994 and now lives in Israel working for the Youth Department of the Reform movement. Nick graduated from Bath University in Business Administration, lives in Birmingham and works as a Marketing Executive in the advertising industry; he married Julie Green in 1994 and their first son Alexander (our first grandchild) was born on 17 March 1996. Simon has become a world traveller. He spent a year in the South African mining industry on a scholarship from De Beers/Oppenheimer (no relation), completed a degree in Mining Engineering at Imperial College in London, toured the USA and Australia, obtained a Master's Degree in Geophysics at Birmingham University and now prospects for oil in Holland (after Pakistan, China, Egypt and Nigeria). He is based in the centre of Birmingham – ideal for all-night parties.

In the meantime, Corinne had become chairman of our synagogue and a senior member of the Solihull magistrates bench, and her teaching career had given way to arranging activities for the elderly residents in the Jewish old-people's home in Stirchley,

CORINNE AND FAMILY

Birmingham. We never spoke German at home and I never talked about Belsen and the Holocaust to our children, until they were well into their teens, even though they may have heard about the subject from other sources. I did not want to worry them or give them sleepless nights, or make them frightened that the Gestapo might arrest them. Corinne and others may not have agreed with me at the time, but our children have learnt about the Holocaust subsequently, and I sincerely hope that they have not been affected in any way by my experiences during the war.

I believe myself lucky not to have been physically or mentally affected by these experiences. I realise now that I had a very interrupted education, attending nine different schools in three different countries with three different languages between 1935 and 1945. I never really learned the grammar of any language, and my vocabulary tends to be limited. I completely missed adolescence and the normal life of a teenager. Between the formative ages of 13 to 17, I never went to a cinema or a dance, I never had a date or met members of the opposite sex. I never went to a concert or visited a museum. In consequence, I never learned to understand and appreciate any forms of art, literature, poetry and music, and I am seriously culturally challenged. This has never been a great obstacle in my life, as I made up for it by spending more time at sports. However, it is beginning to show up in my later life in retirement. For example, I left Germany when I was seven years old; obviously I could speak fluent German, but I knew little about the grammar. When I helped my sons with their German homework 40 years later, I could easily advise them what was right and what was wrong but I could never explain why anything was wrong. And sometimes I confuse the various languages. For example, there is one expression that I will never understand: 'half ten' means 10.30 in this country, but 9.30 in Germany and Holland. I have had many enjoyable arguments with my children about this expression. The English 'double negative' is another mystery that I have not come to terms with: "Don't you like it here?" Do I say "yes" or "no" if I do like it here? My Japanese friends have never understood this expression either, but they answer "yes" to all questions anyway.

Therapists and psychologists may offer other explanations as to why I preferred not to speak German at home, or talk about the Holocaust, and as to why I was always anxious to erase any traces of my German origins. They would probably disagree that I consider myself perfectly normal, on the basis that none of my friends and acquaintances in Birmingham ever noticed or remarked that I was in any way different from them. Furthermore, none of them ever questioned my background. Some friends may have suspected that I came from continental Europe, but no one knew that I had been in Belsen. My only character defect that I would happily blame on the Holocaust is my lasting passion for 'organising' such as the collecting of 'souvenirs'. This was reinforced during my time at university and culminated in my collection of airline cutlery: we have more BA teaspoons than British Airways!

My work at Lucas Girling involved much overseas travelling, which included a year in Japan. In 1970 there was another step-change in my life, when I was appointed to manage the braking regulations standards at Lucas Girling. 20 years later, I was recognised as the 'guru' on braking regulations (a big fish in a small pond) and this led to the award of the MBE in the 1990 New Year's Honours List.

PART SIX

INTO RETIREMENT

Beyond my dreams

Photo: Ruzzi and I at the Belsen Documentation Centre, 1990

INVESTITURE

Buckingham Palace, 13 March 1990

I have now come full circle to the beginning of the book.

I was standing face to face with Her Majesty the Queen. This was my magic moment.

I had ordered the morning dress a few days before, complete with top hat and gloves. Corinne bought a new dress and a new hat. We had been looking forward to the Big Day, although with some apprehension as I was not used to mixing in such circles.

We had arrived outside Buckingham Palace in good time, but disappointed to find out that Simon could have acted as our chauffeur. The three children had drawn straws to see who would go in, as only two were allowed to accompany us into the Palace. If Simon had been our driver, he could have taken us into the Inner Quadrangle and he could have waited for us there inside the Palace grounds, away from the tourists at the front gates. Instead, we had arranged to meet Simon after the ceremony, for a photo session by the Palace gates, with the *Solihull Times* photographer, who would accompany us to Belsen during the following month.

The guests, including Corinne, Nick and Judith, were guided on a very interesting tour of the Palace. In those days there were no visitor tours of the Palace and of course, no souvenir shops. They finished up in the magnificent Ballroom with huge chandeliers and red velvet carpets. The Ballroom had been prepared to seat about 500 visitors, who were entertained by various regimental bands. For most of them, it would be one of the greatest and most memorable days of their lives – and even more so for the individual recipients of honours.

One by one, our names were called by the Lord Chamberlain. When I heard "Oppenheimer", I moved forward smartly, executed a right-angle turn, paused, bowed from the neck, and approached Her Majesty the Queen. Unfortunately, I was so pre-occupied in co-ordinating my hand and foot movements, that I did not hear the rest of the announcement, the only time that they ever explained why I received the MBE: "Mr Paul Oppenheimer, MBE for Services to Industry", Corinne told me afterwards.

Her Majesty the Queen lobbed the medal onto a black plastic hook, which had been fitted to my jacket some hours earlier. There was no messing about with safety pins and there was no blood.

"Congratulations. What do you do?" she enquired. "My wife always asks me that same question," I wanted to say, but this time I had been well briefed by Corinne. "I work on international safety standards for road vehicles, Your Majesty," I answered. "How interesting," she replied, and before I could say any more, she reached out to shake my hand. We had been told that this was the signal that the 'interview' was finished, so I shook hands with Her

INVESTITURE

Majesty the Queen and retreated backwards, rather hastily, trying to remember the pre-programmed steps, bowed again, attempted the reverse turn and left the Ballroom in some disarray.

Little did the Queen realise that I had been a child survivor of Belsen and that I had just completed my journey, not quite from rags to riches, but from the depths of humanity to the pinnacle of success, from Belsen to Buckingham Palace.

Corinne and our children were able to share the wonderful occasion with me. I know my parents would have been so proud of my achievements. But sadly, they were absent.

A NEW PURPOSE

Belsen and beyond.... April 1990 –

Six weeks later, on 22 April 1990, Judith, Ruzzi and I visited
Belsen for the 45th Anniversary of the liberation of the camp.

Today's entrance to the Belsen Memorial site is conveniently
close to the main road from Bergen to Winsen, with a large car
park and an impressive entrance area housing the new
documentation centre. There is an exhibition area in the entrance
hall, a lecture theatre for presentations, a seminar room, a library
and offices. An adjoining annexe displays the infamous period of
the Nazi terror in Germany and the history of the concentration
camps from 1933 to 1945. Of particular interest to me was the scale
model of the original Belsen concentration camp. I never realised
how big it was (much larger than the present Memorial site) and
how many different areas there were. Furthermore, our Barracks
11 is at the very edge of the site, well into the wooded areas. We
found pine trees, 50 feet high, growing in the middle of our
barracks.

FROM BELSEN TO BUCKINGHAM PALACE

A pair of massive iron gates lead to a clearing in the woods, the site of the original camp, with several pathways connecting the few places of interest to be seen today. Dominating the entire Belsen Memorial site is a huge obelisk and 'inscription wall' erected by the British Military Government in 1946. The wall carries many moving messages in many languages including Hebrew, Polish and German. The single English sentence reads:

"To the memory of all those who died in this place".

There is also a separate Jewish Monument, erected on the First Anniversary of the liberation, which reads in Hebrew and English:

"Israel and the world shall remember thirty thousand Jews exterminated in the concentration camp of Bergen-Belsen at the hands of the murderous Nazis. Earth conceal not the blood shed on thee."

And then there are the mass graves – mounds of earth, shaped like bunkers, each with a single inscription in stone. There are a dozen such mass graves, scattered around the site, with up to 9,000 corpses per grave. There is also a large wooden cross, as there were many non-Jewish victims of Belsen, particularly from Poland.

Finally, a small number of individual headstones punctuate the heathland, mainly near the Jewish Monument. Most of these 'symbolic tombstones' (there are no bodies actually buried in that spot) are inscribed in Hebrew or German. Ruzzi and I decided to commission such a headstone in memory of our parents – as individuals, rather than with the anonymous mass graves. We returned to Belsen in September 1992 to consecrate our memorial near the Jewish Monument.

We met an elderly gentleman from London, who had been a barber at Belsen, who saw my brother Ruzzi for the first time in 45 years. He immediately recognised us from Barracks 11 in the *Sternlager* (Star Camp), "I remember your father; is he here?"

A NEW PURPOSE

This incident may be relevant to the trials of surviving German war criminals – everything may depend on the memory and evidence of the witnesses, and our incident shows that there are people who can still remember the daily routines, the special events and the faces from more than 50 years ago. Unfortunately, this elderly gentleman died at home in London just a few months after our reunion.

Parties of schoolchildren and groups of German military personnel were arriving, to be conducted around the site and the exhibition. Apparently, a visit to the site or a concentration camp such as Belsen or Dachau is a compulsory part of their education. A number of local German guides from the voluntary *Besucherdienst* (Visitor Service) are always available at short notice. An amazing 400,000 people visited the Belsen site during the previous year (approximately 1,000 per day). Many British servicemen and their families, from the nearby British Army camps, are also regular visitors to the Belsen Memorial site.

Why did we embark on this pilgrimage to Belsen and rekindle all those terrible memories? On the flight back from Germany, we received a free copy of the *London Evening Standard*. On page five was a story about a spray gas attack on a group of Jewish schoolchildren outside a synagogue in London.... Unfortunately, it is necessary to remember Belsen and to tell the story to more people, and especially to children, who have not heard or seen it, so that it should never happen again.... Ever.

After our return home, there were photographs and stories in the local newspapers, with quotations from Judith:

"Belsen is no longer just a paragraph in a history book; it was important for me to go there, but I cannot really grasp what went on there; I have seen Belsen, but I cannot put it into words."

FROM BELSEN TO BUCKINGHAM PALACE

Our synagogue asked me to give a talk about my 'Return to Belsen', but they also wanted to hear my actual experiences of Belsen during the war. During questions, afterwards, I was amazed to find another Belsen survivor in the audience and three other members of our synagogue who had been in Belsen with the British Army in 1945.

Forty-five years later, when I was explaining our survival in Belsen to a synagogue *Oneg*[2], I met Regina Franks from Coventry. She had been evacuated from Auschwitz to Bergen-Belsen, and they often wondered who those people with yellow stars were. When our compound was suddenly evacuated, Regina feared the worst. It was only at that *Oneg* that Regina found out who was in that compound and what had happened to us. Sadly, Regina Franks died in the spring of 1996.

This proved to be a recurring experience whenever I gave my talk about Belsen to local Rotary clubs and church groups. There were always ex-servicemen who had been in Belsen after the liberation and who wanted to know what it was like before. The newspaper articles about our trip also elicited mail from people who had liberated Belsen or who had been there in 1945. One day, a total stranger who had been a member of the King's Hussars telephoned. Harry Drummond remembered reaching Belsen in 1945, ahead of the 11th Armoured Division and the rest of the advancing British Army. He now lives less than three miles from my home in Solihull and we are good friends and meet regularly.

Soon I was invited to speak to college students and to schoolchildren. The Holocaust became a compulsory part of the history curriculum in English secondary schools and this opened up a whole new series of speaking engagements. Suddenly, people wanted to hear the stories of the survivors of the Holocaust. My

[2]An *Oneg* is a traditional Jewish Friday night gathering to welcome the Sabbath. '*Oneg* Shabbat' literally means 'rejoicing in the Sabbath'.

talks are usually limited to 45 minutes or one hour, supplemented by video footage from the Belsen archives.

This interest was accelerated by films about the Holocaust, notably Steven Spielberg's *Schindler's List*, exhibitions about the Holocaust such as the 'Anne Frank in the World' travelling exhibition and the creation of new Holocaust museums, such as the Holocaust Memorial Museum in Washington DC and the Beth Shalom Holocaust Memorial and Education Centre in Laxton near Nottingham.

After my return to Belsen in 1990, I accepted early retirement from my business commitments and I began to meet other survivors, initially at the Hendon Survivors' Centre. I have also recorded my testimony for the British Video Archives for Holocaust Testimonies, for the Survivors of the Shoah Visual History Foundation, and for the Beth Shalom Holocaust Centre.

My return to Belsen and subsequent events have given me a new purpose in life. I look forward to continuing my association with Beth Shalom and other Holocaust institutions.

THE THREE OPPENHEIMERS
A family story

The period of persecution and incarceration throughout the war
was something which we experienced as a family. We were
fortunate insofar as we were able to stay together much of the time
and were there for each other in times of illness and death. But in
the end, the Nazi regime claimed our parents and all four
grandparents, and sheer good fortune kept us from becoming
victims ourselves.   As a result we are survivors, which
unfortunately, is no claim to fame. We carry no stigma, but neither
is it an honourable status to have. Circumstances bestowed it on
us and we now have to live with it. As brothers and sister, what
affected one of us, affected all three of us in one way or another
during the period of the Holocaust itself. Afterwards we each had
to plough our own furrow and make the best of our situations. I
have already mentioned my own story of my return to society and,
one would hope, normality. I would now like to take up the last

few pages to mention my brother and sister, to whom I remain as close and as dedicated as ever.

Eve was the youngest of the three of us and, of course, the reason for our eventual survival. However, she was still only a child during our years of captivity. She has told me many times of the fear she felt as a little girl, bewildered by the ominous circumstances. She remembers little about the camps themselves, but does remember vividly being terrified by the uniforms of the SS and other guards. To her, this authority was dangerous and frightening. She had the feeling of being lost and did not know what was happening to her, especially after Mother's death. One of her few clear memories of Belsen is the time when Father sat her on one of the bunks in the barracks and told her that Mother had died. She did not remember Father's death. Eve was quickly adopted by the Birnbaums who cared for her welfare as best they could. Interestingly, Eve does not remember them or what they did for her. It appears she was still very bewildered by the deaths of our parents and the rapid change of circumstances as we were shunted around Europe on the 'Last Train'. Neither does she remember being separated from us, or our fortunate reunion at Leipzig.

Eve loved Tante Fie. It is always difficult to say, but she was probably not ready to be plunged into life in England so soon after her ordeal in the camps. Time is needed to adjust to a sense of normality after such events, and that was not a luxury she could have, as her closest family members felt responsible for her well-being. Uncle Rudi became her guardian and she stayed with him and Aunt Lotte in London until 1950, when she was sent to boarding school in Hove. Eve really hated the environment in school. Everyone had families and a normal existence, which was to be expected, but nobody made the effort to understand her unusual and tragic life. She was lonely in every sense of the word, although both Ruzzi and I would visit as often as we could.

Soon after, Eve was accepted into the Lingfield House children's home. This was a most remarkable home for 24 children who came to England in 1945/46. Most of them had been rescued from the concentration camps, but there were also some who had been 'hidden' children. The home was run by Alice Goldberger, a wonderful lady, loved and admired by all who knew her. The children were encouraged to lead normal lives, and they received lots of love and care to help them to gain the strength to cope with future years. There were already two girls called Eve, and so our Eve used her other name Rachel, which has stuck with her friends in London. Even today she keeps in touch with some of the now elderly carers, who meant so much to her at that time.

From Lingfield House, Eve started working for Uncle Rudi at Astra Gloves in the West End and moved to the Sarah Pike hostel and eventually to her own flat in Highgate. She continued working for Uncle Rudi's firm until 1982. Like many survivors, she kept in touch with the few people who had shared and understood her experiences. In 1990, she went to a reunion of former Lingfield House children in America as part of the First International Conference of Child Survivors of the Holocaust held in Los Angeles. She greatly appreciated the occasion and she has since attended many similar functions. She also regularly meets with other child survivors. Eve now works for the Jewish Community and is actively involved in her synagogue. Eve does not make a point of talking about her experiences, but she is very keen that our story is told and earnestly hopes that Holocaust education will continue to develop.

FROM BELSEN TO BUCKINGHAM PALACE

Ruzzi was always the adventurer. Alert, quick-witted and intelligent, he sensed danger and used his natural abilities to avoid it getting the better of him. He was also tremendously inventive, finding ways of trying to help the whole family from an early age. Even in Westerbork, when he was just 12 years old, he was watching what was going on around him and learning the art of survival. Mother kept a tight rein on him in Westerbork, as he was still staying in the women's barracks. However, in Belsen he was housed in the men's barracks and had much more freedom to deploy his skills. We are deeply indebted to him for his persistence in trying to find the best means of survival in the camp. Whether it was in finding extra rations or attempting to organise certain privileges, he was always active on our behalf.

On our arrival in England, Ruzzi remained with Uncle Rudi for a while before moving to our mother's cousin, who lived a couple of miles away, where he stayed for over a year. He then moved to the Meyer family, who were close friends of Uncle Rudi and Aunt Lotte, where he stayed throughout the rest of his high school and university years. Ruzzi also became an engineer, studying at Imperial College London, from where he graduated with a degree in electrical engineering in 1953. After serving a two-year apprenticeship with BTH in Rugby, he went overseas to work for Shell in The Hague in Holland, eventually moving into his own house in Wassenaar. He worked for Shell for 34 years, spending time on overseas assignments, including several years in Venezuela.

Ruzzi is now retired and has returned to England. Like myself he recognises the importance of making our story accessible to as many young people as possible and intends to make a concerted effort to speak and teach as much as possible.

THE THREE OPPENHEIMERS

According to Dr Thomas Rahe, the historian and director at the Belsen Documentation Centre: *"Close to 3,000 children under the age of 15 were taken to Bergen-Belsen, more than any other concentration camp. It is not known exactly how many were still alive at the liberation, but they will be the last survivors of the camps, the last to be able to testify."*

Ruzzi and I were between 11 and 16 years old in Westerbork and Bergen-Belsen; old enough to appreciate what was going on, and old enough to remember it. But we did not record our experiences at the time and almost never talked about those days during 40 years or more. We never appreciated that our eyewitness accounts might be important. Now, time is of the essence as our memory is fading, and we struggle to remember.

Today, all three of us remain committed to explaining our experiences and trying to ensure that it was not all in vain. It can never be a happy end, because the loss of our home and the destruction of all our loved ones cannot be undone. The Nazi years are over. We no longer have to look over our shoulders, or fear uniforms, or consider how to get the most out of our next meagre ration. We live in better times. However, we feel the necessity to reflect on the past, not for old times' sake, nor for the exorcising of memories perhaps best left alone, but because we care about the future.

THE BIRDS OF BELSEN

When Richard Dimbleby returned to the Belsen camp in 1959, he observed something which many people have repeated to me since:

"Do you know what is strange about this place? There isn't a single bird singing here."

Well, the birds are singing again, even at Belsen. The world has to go on living. The entire area of the former camp has been landscaped so that it resembles something of a beautiful parkland, totally unrecognisable as one of the most notorious concentration camps of the Second World War.

Nothing is left of the stench of rotting corpses. Now only the memory remains, and we who bear it. We can only say what we saw and hope that it means something to you. One cannot imagine the filth, the fear, or the horror of those years which are, thankfully, behind us. It is a world which, though we hope it will never be witnessed again, we must nevertheless try to understand.

Perhaps this book will help....

Paul Oppenheimer 1996

APPENDICES

Appendix 1

Five generations of Oppenheimers.

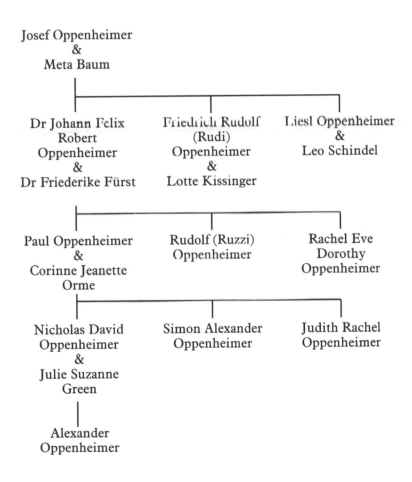

Josef Oppenheimer
&
Meta Baum

Dr Johann Felix Robert Oppenheimer & Dr Friederike Fürst

Friedrich Rudolf (Rudi) Oppenheimer & Lotte Kissinger

Liesl Oppenheimer & Leo Schindel

Paul Oppenheimer & Corinne Jeanette Orme

Rudolf (Ruzzi) Oppenheimer

Rachel Eve Dorothy Oppenheimer

Nicholas David Oppenheimer & Julie Suzanne Green

Simon Alexander Oppenheimer

Judith Rachel Oppenheimer

Alexander Oppenheimer

Appendix 2

Extracts from Yad Vashem Archives.

Oppenheimer,	19-10-1866	Kleinwallstadt
Josef	23-07-1943	Sobibor
Oppenheimer-Baum,	10-02-1876	Nuremberg
Meta	23-07-1943	Sobibor
Fürst,	01-09-1865	Heidelberg
Rudolf	26-03-1943	Sobibor
Fürst-Oppé,	03-10-1875	Mühlhausen
Hedwig	26-03-1943	Sobibor
Oppenheimer,	18-06-1901	Fürth
Johann Felix Robert	20-03-1945	Bergen-Belsen
Oppenheimer-Fürst,	23-01-1902	Heidelberg
Friederike	17-01-1945	Bergen-Belsen

Appendix 3

Translation of a postcard from my father in Berlin addressed to his brother, Rudi, in London.

24 March 1936

My loved ones,

We hope that Lotte is fully recovered, so that you are quite fit for the visitors. The three of them* will depart this evening and expect that you will receive them at 16.20 at Victoria. I am sorry, from all points of view, that I cannot be with them, but the thought of seeing such a longstanding wish fulfilled, is already wonderful and really sufficient.

To you, I wish that the three will cause minimal disturbance, perhaps as much cannot be avoided, whilst you derive also some pleasure.

With sincerest thanks,

Your H. (Hans)

* My mother, Ruzzi and me. We would be travelling by train and boat from Berlin via Ostend and Dover to London Victoria Station.

Appendix 4

Translation of a letter from Westerbork, 1943.

Letter from my mother in Barracks 65 in Westerbork, to Mrs S. Koster in Amsterdam, written in pencil on the original Westerbork camp stationery, and stamped by the censor.

Dear Tante Fie,

The latest rules offer fewer opportunities to write and we have to 'ration' our messages severely. But from one or other of our acquaintances, you will surely have heard, that we are doing relatively well; we hope that with you everything is also healthy and in good order. You will surely have heard about the new rules for parcels; we are only permitted to receive parcels from family and Jewish acquaintances, which must be accompanied by a label, as enclosed; the weight must not be more than 2 kg. It is best to stitch the label securely inside the top of the parcel, so that it will not be lost and will be found immediately when it is opened. We would be pleased to receive another of those bottles of shampoo such as you sent us previously, and if possible, some porridge oats (raw) for the children. Otherwise, anything is of course welcome. Now, we wish you all the very best for the forthcoming holidays and for the New Year. Let us hope that at last, it will bring peace for all of us. With best regards, also from the children,
always yours,
> *Frieda.*

N.B. This letter was posted on 24 December 1943.

Aunt Lotte and Uncle Rudi on their 50th wedding
anniversary, 1984

Ruzzi, Eve and I by the memorial we placed at
Belsen in memory of our parents, 1995

The MBE medal presented to me by
Her Majesty the Queen

Left to right: Simon, Corinne, Judith and Nick with me outside the Palace, 1990

Ruzzi, Judith and I at the Jewish Memorial, Bergen Belsen, 1990

The family, left to right:
Simon, Corinne, Ruzzi, Judith, Eve, Nick and I

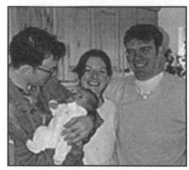

My children (and grandchild) left to right:
Simon, Alexander, Judith and Nick

The 'ramp' at Belsen. This is where we were loaded and
unloaded. It is over two miles from the camp itself

The first time Ruzzi and I returned to Belsen in 1953 we travelled
across Europe by motorbike

Ruzzi (right), Eve and I in the 1960s